CUSTOM RIDES

THE COOLEST MOTORCYCLE BUILDS AROUND THE WORLD

ROBERT DAVIES

The History Press

First published 2018

The History Press
The Mill, Brimscombe Port
Stroud, Gloucestershire, GL5 2QG
www.thehistorypress.co.uk

British Library Cataloguing in Publication Data.
A catalogue record for this book is available from the British Library.

ISBN 978 0 7509 8380 8

Typesetting and origination by The History Press
Printed and bound in India by Thomson Press India Ltd

Front cover: Graphite Speedster from Rough Crafts Winston Yeh.
Back cover, left to right: Typhoon from Old Empire Motorcycles,
Honda CB900F in café racer trim from 2WheelsMiklos,
BMW R75/5 from 6/5/4 Motors.

CONTENTS

Acknowledgements	6
Introduction	7
Chicara Nagata – The Motorcycle Artist (Japan/USA/M.A.D. Gallery, Switzerland)	15
Rough Crafts Winston Yeh (Taiwan/USA)	21
Sinroja (UK)	53
Tricana (France/Switzerland)	67
Martyn Wilkins (UK)	73
2WheelsMiklos (Spain/UK)	83
6/5/4 Motors (Sweden)	97
Diamond Atelier (Germany)	107
Max Hazan (USA)	117
it roCkS! Bikes (Portugal)	123
Lorne Cheetham's Kickback Custom Bike Show (UK)	129
Old Empire Motorcycles (UK)	133
Raccia Motorcycles (USA)	143
Auto Fabrica (India/UK)	153
Ludovic Lazareth (France)	157

ACKNOWLEDGEMENTS

My grateful thanks to all the wonderful people that contributed freely of their time, photographs and information that went into the making of this book. Many, from all over the world, responded as though they had known me for years, sending more photographs than I could ever use. The bikes range from the fantastic, right through to the sort of bike that you would love to jump on and ride every day. If I have made any mistakes – and there are always a few – then I apologise profusely with the hope that the rest of the book will make up for this. For me, this work has been an education, and I have the simple hope that you will love the bikes within these covers just as much as I did when I first saw them.

Robert Davies, 2017

INTRODUCTION

Do you love motorcycles? Do you love beautiful motorcycles? Then you'll definitely love the bikes in this book. Feast your eyes and eat your heart out for all the bikes you would love to have and own but can't possibly afford. Oh you can, can you? Lucky devil.

For most people, motorcycles are a Marmite thing; either you love them or you don't. But many of us developed that love in our early years, and it's a connection between man and machine that never leaves the soul. As a wise man once said: 'Cars move the body, but motorcycles move the heart.' So, if you have never experienced the thrill, the sheer joy, of weaving your way in the fluid motion that only two wheels and a responsive engine can give, along a fabulous road, past glorious scenery, with the warmth of the sun on your body and the wind gently tugging at your clothes, then I truly feel sorry for you. For there is simply nothing quite like it.

When singer Avril Lavigne wrote in one of her punchier and angst-ridden songs about wanting to be anything but ordinary please, she may well have been writing for all of those guys beavering away in their sheds to produce their unique motorcycles. In this book I have tried to include as many gorgeous bikes from as many distant parts of the world as possible but you can never include them all as there are so many. Some of the companies are well-established thriving businesses, and they have produced some amazing two-wheeled dream machines. Most start small and stay small, but that in no way diminishes the level of sophistication of their product. And that is exactly what guys like Martyn Wilkins have produced in his first real attempt to manufacture his own take on the Café Racer scene. There has always been an underground movement to individualise one's machine, but in recent years this movement has increased, and not just from the traditional areas such as the UK, America and Europe, but also ironically from the heartland of the mass modern production bike – Japan. Martyn happens to be a friend of mine and doesn't live too far away, so I have been fortunate to be able to follow his builds. As for Winston Yeh in Taiwan, I just love what he does. He is amazing, but I can't afford to jet off all over the world and meet these amazing designers, more's the pity. So I will have to stick to my emails and foster good relationships in the electronic media. It is nowhere near as good as meeting people face-to-face, but what else can you do?

But what about Japan's stock output? Has the country's large production of frankly fantastic stock machines affected what is happening in the custom scene today? The answer is a firm 'yes', for the big four have simply provided more machines from which custom designers can create their own individual styles; a blank canvas in effect. And, oddly enough, there has been something of a minor but noticeable backlash against the factory-produced machine by a growing section of the motorcycling fraternity who want something individual and different from the rest of the herd. Not happy with all the latest features, styling and complexity of the factory machine, they wish to make their own bikes with a distinctive style born out of a combination of the creative urge and desire to be different.

Ironically, in recent years some of the big guys, or the original equipment manufacturers (OEMs) as we label them, in order to attract a younger audience have turned to these tiny companies to tap into the artistic flood of talent – the spirit of the age – so as to create the bikes that people want to ride. Some, like Yamaha for instance, have handed over stock bikes, plus a wad of cash, and given the smaller designers free rein in the creative department, and these guys have come up with the goods. Closely connected, of course, is the way that the Internet has changed the world of motorcycling as it has other walks of life. In my youth during the 1960s there was no Internet, no computers, no catalogues to consult; you could only turn to your local bike shops for ideas, and a small choice of parts.

Take a look at my initial thrust into customising, the chopped A10 that I did in about 1971. Don't look for too long though as it's a bit embarrassing. In those crazy, exciting days of fast-moving music and fashion there was no social media, no mobile phones, and no catalogues of parts that you could choose from. I was able to get a 12in pair of overstock forks but I didn't have the skill to cut and re-weld the steering head, so that had to do. I made a pair of extended footrests with their attachments of gear change and brake, and that was a start. You had never heard of powder coating then, so I had the frame stove enamelled,

a large rim laced to the rear wheel, and a car tyre on that (a small rim for the front and a chromed BSA hub). Actually very tasty. I fitted a central oil tank which was copper plated; it was different and looked fab (now there's a 1960s word you don't hear today). A tuck and roll seat on a wide mudguard, and it was pretty well there. Personally I was never in love with ape hangers, which were much too common. I much preferred my rather cool Z bars.

When I rode that bike around the English Black Country I thought I was king of the road. Oh, and by the way, I just about caught the last few years when you didn't have to wear a crash helmet. Of course, I can see the wisdom of wearing a lid, and I have no doubt, and the statistics will prove conclusively, that crash helmets have saved countless lives. But, to be able to ride around in the summer, without the stuffiness of having a lid on was not just liberating, it was freedom, and wonderful all at the same time. Only the other day I went on to some private land and rode around without my full-face crash helmet and savoured the wind around my head. It was a heady mix of nostalgia and sheer exhilaration. But that's another topic entirely, and the crash helmet law is here to stay, and it's a good one.

From the 1950s through to the 1970s, most bikers just wanted to make their ride go that little bit faster than the stock model and performed what we called in ye olde days 'hotting it up', which included fitting higher lift cams, higher compression pistons and polishing the inlet and exhaust ports for better gas flow. Many lowered the handlebars of their chosen mount with the historic Ace or clip-ons in order to cut wind resistance and emulate their heroes from the Isle of Man TT Races. Others simply removed all the stuff that got in the way, such as heavy mudguards and lighting systems, and rode them

My 'chopped' A10 in 1971.

wherever it was possible. Over the years various styles of bike racing came into being. In the US, bikes were hurled around banked boarded tracks, others preferred to stay on grass. Guys wishing to go on longer journeys and desiring to look cool at the same time, extended their forks, made forward foot controls for relaxed riding, and in the US the 'chopper' was born.

So today we have a rich legacy of what can loosely be called 'bike fashions' to choose from that include chops, brats, bobbers, street scramblers, board trackers and, perhaps the coolest and increasingly popular style, the café racer, to which several books and at least two YouTube channels are devoted. So there again, the Internet has had a huge influence on what is possible, and there has been a flood of online blogs dedicated to every kind of bike you can imagine, and some you can't, so that a whole biking subculture has emerged that the large manufacturers would like to tap in to.

Some companies such as Deus Ex Machina are not only making bikes but encouraging potential purchasers into their in-house coffee shops, and they are selling a lifestyle with their own branded jeans, T-shirts, shoes, etc., that in some instances makes more cash than the bike sales. I know, it's an odd but a fascinating world, and that includes the brave entrepreneur John Bloor, who has reinvigorated the Triumph brand. He has not missed a trick in this department either and the company is producing a whole raft of merchandise that takes in clothing and bolt-on goodies for its latest bikes such as the recent bobbed Bonnevilles and more futuristic triples.

I went into my local store to buy a couple of magazines the other day and counted eight devoted to one form of biking or other. They are heavily augmented by very popular websites such as Pipeburn, BikExif and Sump, which publish really cutting edge journalism and pictures that fire the imagination and greatly influence a younger audience. And then there are us older guys who are still heavily supporting the world of motorcycling. At the café to where I often ride, a popular biking haunt at Quatt near beautiful rural Bridgnorth, it's often crowded with an experienced set of what I would call mature riders, over 50s and even 80s bless 'em, that sit there with a bacon sarnie and cuppa dispensing spannering wisdom and associated biking tales. On the weekends, a younger crowd of bikers fill the car park with their well-loved machines that range from an R1 to a Harley, kicking out their side stand to see and be seen. It's with the influence of the Internet that the younger generation have again seen that bikes are cool and desirable. Some, of course, covet and then buy the fastest sport bike that they can afford. However, a completely different crowd desire a bike that diffuses the younger spirit of fun, rebellion, wildness, whatever you want to call it, to make their own mark on the world around them. This is the Alternative Custom scene, or Alt.com, and it's here to stay, grow and evolve.

Certainly café racers as a style are not a new phenomenon, for they are an echo from the Britain of the 1950s and '60s. It was an era when groups of leather-clad youths with their own language and music hurtled from café to café in pursuit of the elusive 'ton'. In those days, a 650 was a *big* bike (not any more) that included the Triumphs, BSAs and Nortons. However in 1969, a seminal movie came out that had a big impact and influence on many of us. It was called *Easy Rider*.

For those of you who were fortunate enough to miss that basically dreadful film, spawned from a mind-bending decade of immense social change that threw every kind of morality to the four winds, I will give you the bare bones. *Easy Rider* has oft been described as a modern Western, whatever that means, whereby the two main characters have swapped their four-legged steeds for a couple of glitzy Harley-Davidson choppers. In essence the film was a reflection, nay glorification, of the drug-fuelled, free love society that had recently mushroomed as a kind of rebellion following the austerity and death-filled years of the Second World War and its successor, the Vietnam War (that was still ongoing). There was a nod to the cowboy movie genre because the two main characters, played by Peter Fonda and Dennis Hopper, were called Wyatt and Billy, thus recalling the famed Wyatt Earp and Billy the Kid. In the movie, Fonda in patriotic irony wears a stars and stripes flag on his jacket, while Hopper is decked out in Native American buckskin.

In the explosive and dramatic finale, and maybe there is a kind of moral conclusion at the end, the two main characters are murdered right before they deliver some drugs and make their money. And then the credits roll.

Just one of my many replicas.

The movie quickly became a global hit, more thanks to its real main characters – the bikes – plus its fabulous pounding music and lyrics, provided by Jimi Hendrix, The Band and The Byrds. And who cannot now fail to recall the heart-thumping start to 'Born to be Wild' by Steppenwolf? The movie grossed millions of dollars and broke ground by being one of the first to use popular music instead of an orchestrated background. In fact, without the dramatic soundtrack, it would have been a tedious tale of two guys riding around on a couple of flashy bikes and breaking the law. Nevertheless, the last song mentioned alone sold over a million copies and was awarded a gold disc. I know, there wasn't much of a story, but it did seem to capture the spirit of the age. However, as I mentioned earlier, the bikes were the real interest. But where did those fantastic and now legendary custom bikes come from?

They were Harley-Davidson hard tail frames and panhead engines, designed and built by two African–American chopper builders, Cliff Vaughns and Ben Hardy, with artistic ideas coming from Fonda. Four ex-police bikes were used in the film, bought in an auction for a reputed $500, where each bike had a backup in case of an accident. There seems to be a bit of mystery of what happened to the bikes after filming. Apparently three were stolen, never to be seen again, while one ended up for a while in a motorcycle museum in Anamosa, Iowa. Fortunately for me, an exact replica came into the café at Bridgnorth during the month that I was writing the introduction to this book, so you can get a look at a pretty good replica of Fonda's legendary machine. Don't forget, of course, that for a modern road bike, there are certain later additions, such as a disc brake up front, so please try not to nit-pick.

Clifford Vaughns (1937–2016) was a black civil rights activist; ex US marine, film-maker, and I don't know how he did it but he still found time to design some really cool motorcycles for which he never really received the credit. Vaughns was working as an associate producer for *Easy Rider* when he commissioned his pal, Ben Hardy, to build the two leading bikes. I did read that it was also Vaughns who suggested the title for the film, the phrase coming from a 1913 Ragtime tune recorded by Mae West in 1933, and the easy rider in question was a horse and not a motorcycle.

The history of choppers as a motorcycling style is covered superbly in a book by Paul d'Orleans, a long-time experienced motorcycle scribe, who in an article in a UK-based magazine, *Classic Bike Guide* (September 2015) asked the question: 'Is there art in motorcycles? In that article d'Orleans mentions the work of Chicara Nagata, a genius in the alchemy of turning beautiful metallic shapes into motorcycles (more of his creations later on). Ultimately the reader alone must decide whether Nagata's bikes are for riding on or simply admiring and attaching to a wall as you would a work of art. For me, d'Orleans hits the nail on the head when he writes the succinct philosophy that: 'It's what moves us that moves us.' So in essence, for a bike to be truly beautiful, it needs to be a fully functioning piece of transport where the controls come comfortably to hands and feet, and where it transports its rider wonderfully and majestically through the landscape. Yes we all have our own idea of what is the most perfect and truly beautiful motorcycle but what biker worth his salt cannot be moved by the classic lines of a Vincent, BSA Goldstar, HD 1200 Sportster or Kawasaki Z1?

This book therefore is all about beautiful, amazing and, to be frank, often fantastic motorcycles. We will also be taking a close look at the custom builders' story; the man of ideas who takes a stock bike and using his inherent artistic and learned skills makes someone's dream machine appear. A man who in the twenty-first century has the pinnacle of materials technology at his fingertips, which includes computer-aided design (CAD) and computer numerical construction (CNC) plus the benefits of the Internet for sourcing and purchasing parts, and getting any required knowhow. These guys are dedicated to their craft, put in a phenomenal amount of hours, are skilled at what they do, and are extremely knowledgeable. The end result is a wide array of wonderful motorcycles that display their makers' own unique philosophy of what a motorcycle should be. But if you love bikes, and we all do, then you will appreciate them all. And I can only apologise profusely if your particular piece of pride and joy is not featured within these covers. My only defence, and it's a pretty good one, is that there are too many for one volume. Along with the fabulous photos, I have added detailed build notes for many of the bikes to keep the tech guys happy.

Left: **The iconic fuel tank signed by Fonda himself.**

Above: **The Harley-Davidson engine and gearbox looking its best.**

CHICARA NAGATA – THE MOTORCYCLE ARTIST

I am kicking off with the world of pure fantasy bikes, and why not? So, courtesy of the M.A.D. Gallery in Geneva, I not only have the low-down on this fascinating guy, but some fabulous pictures of his awesome machines, and I thank them profusely for their input to this book. Others may immediately view him as the King of Bling, that is as far as motorcycles are concerned, for his style is somewhere between Cartier and Heath Robinson. But as the M.A.D. Gallery so succinctly put it in its advertising blurb:

> Thinking of Chicara Nagata's motorcycles as a simple means of transportation would be insane. You could ride them, you could perform on the road but, unfortunately, it wouldn't be legally allowed.

I'll leave you to your own ides of what you think of Chicara's bikes, but consider this. Only this year, I witnessed at least one Kawasaki Z1 be purchased as an ornament. It was to have no oil or petrol ever in it; it was therefore never destined to be ridden, but to sit in pride of place in – I'm guessing – a large home. So, if you wished to decorate a room with a motorcycle theme, you couldn't do better than a genuine Chicara – that's if you could afford one of course.

For two decades this unique Japanese artist dedicated his entire energy to the creation of art pieces, most commonly known as motorcycles. He was born in 1962, in the Saga Prefecture of Kyushu Island, eighteen hours away from Tokyo. He says, 'When I was a teenager, I spent all my time gazing at my older friends' motorcycles and wanted to ride one myself,' he continues, 'What I really wanted was to ride a motorcycle that was all my own. That was what gave me the idea to build custom bikes.'

Oddly enough, it was a bike that almost killed him in a terrible accident when he was aged 16, and he spent eight months in hospital fighting for his life. He relates, 'I was told that I would not survive, but here I am still alive today'.

However, he continually wonders why his life was saved while others didn't survive similar accidents. He wanted to reassure the world that he was alive and well by throwing his energy into something he was good at. He decided to use his unique skillset to build the motorcycles that meant so much to him. He then drew, crafted and assembled close to 500 components for a vintage engine, manufactured between 1939 and 1966. The amount of pieces and time spent on each machine gives a completely different dimension to the motorcycle.

Chicara Art One.

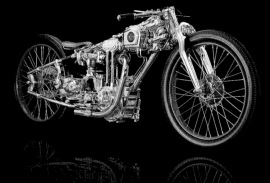

His obsession for detail is amazing, spending nearly three years on the completion of his first piece of art, **Chicara One,** which he finished in 2004 after 7,500 hours of work. Since 2004, his driving ambition has taken the two-wheeled machine to an elevated art form, starting with unique pieces he named **Chicara Art, 1-4.** With these, he has won six consecutive awards at shows in Belgium, France, and Germany, before gaining global recognition at the AMD Championship (the world's most recognised custom bike award). Indeed, like them or disregard them as real motorcycles, you can't deny his huge talent with all metals, and as a consequence he became world champion of custom bike design when he took the first place for Chicara Art One in 2006 and the second place the following year with Chicara Art Two, both in the freestyle class of the AMD.

In 2012, Chicara unveiled three of his extraordinary creations at the M.A.D. Gallery in Geneva: Chicara Art One, Three and Four. The following year he returned to pick up just Chicara Art One and Three as Four had been sold, but in exchange he delivered Chicara Art Five.

He went on to say, 'I need new challenges ... If at all possible, I want to keep making a new work of art each year.'

Above left: **Chicara Nagata.**

Above: **Studio – Chicara Nagata.**

Opposite: **Three pieces of motorcycle art.**

Clockwise: **Engine detail, saddle detail, views from above.**

© Frank Kletschkus– Germany

© Frank Kletschkus- Germany

© Frank Kletschkus- Germany

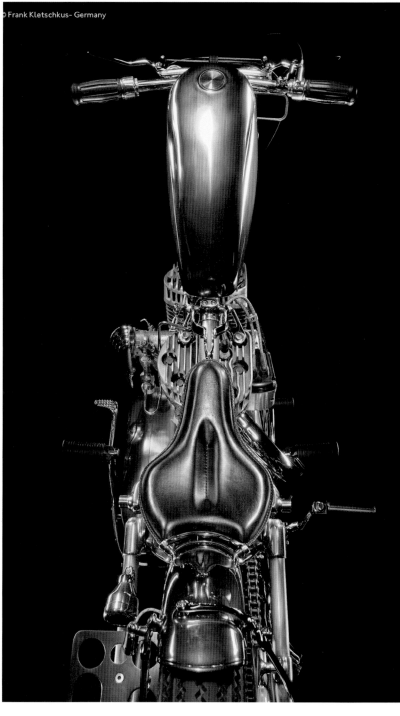

© Frank Kletschkus- Germany

ROUGH CRAFTS WINSTON YEH

TAIWAN/USA

I have to admit that Winston is one of my favourite designers. Though still a young man, he has such a great talent and a natural eye for what makes a truly beautiful bike, so I am going to be indulgent and feature over the next few pages six of his creations. And for the techies among you, I have included the build notes as well as the sumptuous photographs.

Winston Yeh, now back in his home country of Taiwan after a spell in the US where he learned so much, would confirm with a grin that nerdy young kids who play with such mind-stretching toys as Lego Technics, can and will grow to be wildly creative adults. And, since founding his custom bike company back in 2010, Winston has gone on to win some very prestigious awards for his motorcycles.

When a friend at the college of Art and Design in Pasadena, California, bought a flighty Yamaha 150, Winston liked it so much he bought one of his own, and started a lifetime of tinkering with two-wheeled machinery – maybe just like the rest of us. His own break into bike design was a unique journey. While still at college he won an eBay collection of bike parts and promptly drove over to the seller's address to pick them up, only to discover that the building was the headquarters of Performance Machines, the guys who design and make all the bolt-on accessories for Harley-Davidson. The manager, who came out with the parts

in question, asked kindly why a kid would want these parts. So, Winston explained that he was studying art and design at the local college. The manager then wisely and speedily introduced Winston to the head of the design department, the famous Roland Sands, who was intrigued by Winston's attitude. Winston showed Sands some of his designs of graffiti walls that he had done recently, and Sands invited Winston to decorate one of the company's interior walls, as you do. *'Do some art work; anything you like, with that wall over there!'* So Winston took up that challenge and got on with it. They were impressed.

Two weeks later, Winston was invited back to design T-shirts, and ended up working for Performance Machines for the next nine months as graphic designer. During that productive period, he soaked up new information and then took his new skills and knowledge back to his home country of Taiwan. Taiwan has a problem, however, with the making and using of custom machines, and the country's laws are pretty draconian and very restrictive when it comes to any alterations to a stock bike. But Winston was determined to carry on with his heart's desire.

Winston's design philosophy, for motorcycles at any rate, is a simple one, and that is to create harmony where one part of the bike does not overwhelm or stand out from the whole, such as with the paintwork on

Graphite Speedster.

Urban cavalry.

metalwork. He readily admits that he is a poor fabricator or mechanic, much preferring to concentrate on design while hiring the best of those worlds to do their bit for the build process. Very helpfully, Taiwan is a world leader in CNC manufacturing and engineering, so it's pretty easy to look around locally and find a company that is ready and willing to manufacture his designs. Winston also has a mail order side of his company that oversees the selling and delivery of the custom parts that he has had made and featured on his own bikes. Simple, eh?

Winston's company, Rough Crafts, has now built a niche global reputation, receiving praise from those including his former mentor Roland Sands, and also Steve Willis of the British Harley-Davidson shop Speed & Custom. Yes, Winston's bikes have, along with other small concerns, helped to attract a whole new generation into Harley showrooms. It is obvious that he has his own vision of how a motorcycle should look, and uses that to express his creative talents. And – admitting that I have never been a great Harley fan – I like what he does.

Winston Yeh.

Bavarian Fistfighter – Build Notes

Winston's BMW R9T, the Bavarian Fistfighter, is a tribute to past designs, but with a heavy input of modern technology. BMW Motorrad is a brand that has a rich and long history in motorcycling, and one of Rough Crafts' main design aesthetics is to blend the beautiful lines from the past into modern finishing. Winston then considers all of the lines of the machine, takes hints from various old BMW gas tanks, and blends them with his own 'signature style'. The vintage rubber seat inspired his single seat, while the vintage BMW snowflake wheels inspired custom one-off billet CNC wheels and rotors. All these features are combined with modern RnineT inverted forks, Brembo/Beringer brakes, custom rear shock from Gears Racing, and ultra-sticky race slick tyres from Pirelli. Rough Crafts' custom-made velocity stacks and exhausts helps the engine breathe better; this R9T then becomes a showpiece.

Says Winston:

"This collaboration with BMW Motorrad was an interesting affair. I met BMW Motorrad's head of vehicle design, Ola Stenegärd, many times at different bike shows and talked about what we could do together all the time. Then BMW Motorrad Taiwan called without knowing our relationship asking me to build a custom R9T. Naturally, BMW Motorrad Munich jumped on this idea and Thras Papadimitriou at BMW Motorrad put it into one of the officially endorsed Soulfuel nineT builds.

Pirelli Taiwan heard about the build and sponsored us their Diablo Superbike slicks. Gears Racing built us Rough Crafts special R9T rear shock, Beringer Brakes provided the hydraulic hand controls, and Roland Sands Design sent us their engine covers, which turned into Rough Crafts-style finishing to help the complete package.

Once again, 2 Abnormal Sides made us the brass tank badge, and KIC airsoft helped us engrave the BMW logo on the badge. OneHandMade helped all the bodywork, and Motogadget provided the gauge, grips and bar-end turn signals; Sato Racing for the rearsets. Last but not least, Air Runner Custom Paint did a traditional BMW dual stripes paint job but with a twist; carbon fibre fading with dual stripes in silver leafs with shades of black candy to give it more depth."

Bavarian Fistfighter.

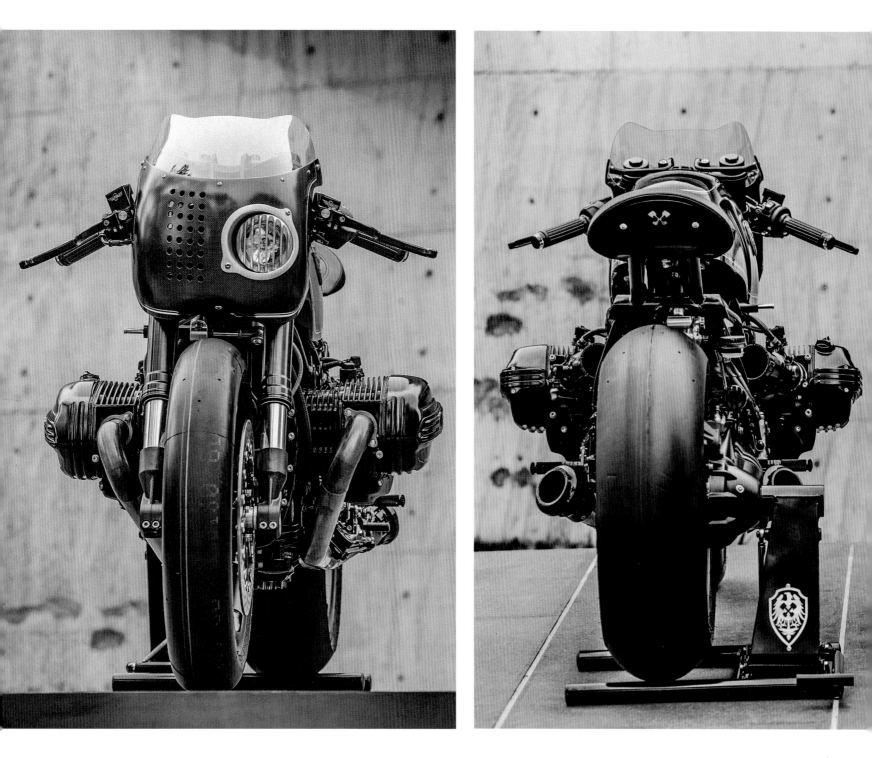

Photo by: JL Photography

Year/Model: 2015

Engine Make/Size: BMW Motorrad/1170cc

Frame Make/Type: Stock with slightly mod under the seat

Front End Make/Type: Stock inverted forks blacked out

Rear Suspension: Rough Crafts/Gears Racing

Rake: Stock

Stretch: None

Swingarm: Stock

Transmission/Drives/Clutch: Stock

Wheels F: Rough Crafts one-off 3.50 × 17in

Wheels R: Rough Crafts one-off 6.00 × 17in

Tyres F: Pirelli Diablo Superbike 120/70 R 17

Tyres R: Pirelli Diablo Superbike 200/60 R 17

Brakes F: Stock Brembo/Rough Crafts one-off matching 330mm discs

Brakes R: Stock BMW

Painter: Air Runner Custom Paint

Foot controls: Sato Racing rear sets

Handlebar controls: Beringer

Headlight: Rough Crafts grille-type headlight

Taillight: Rough Crafts grille-type LED taillight

Seat: Rough Crafts

Gas caps: Rough Crafts

Grips: Motogadget

Engine Covers: Roland Sands Design/Rough Crafts

Graphite Speedster – Build Notes

Winston tells the bike's story:

'The bike was commissioned by Harley-Davidson Taiwan, along with another custom bike they built themselves, and another eight custom-painted bikes for their annual event, to spread out the custom culture in our relatively conservative country.

'It was so unexpected to hear them giving me 100 per cent freedom of design and direction of the bike, so I decided to go the total opposite of what "Harley people" usually expect to see for custom; to reverse usual Harley's heavy, bad stopping and lazy suspension' I decided to go the full performance route, but still trying to keep the "Rough Crafts look" intact. I chose Dyna platform, as I think it's got the good bike size/engine power balance, and potential for good handling among HD model families. Zach Ness from Arlen Ness jumped off first with their latest design of bevelled wheels, classic simple lines perfectly fitting for this with Dunlop street race tyres.

'Paul from Lyndall Racing Brake had been talking with me about working together for quite some time – their all black composite rotors are just extraordinary – and he decided to custom-make me matching rotors for the wheels we had. Now on to suspensions. Satya Kraus from Kraus Moto Co. has been a very good friend of mine for several years; I always loved his Dynamoto Front End kit he combined with Ohlins inverted forks. This was just the perfect opportunity to run it with Ohlins shocks in the back, too.

'For calipers, Gard from LA Chop Rods hooked me up with the finest brake system by ISR brakes, which has a design that is very industrial and simple with top-notch braking power, now on to the engine. As usual, 2 Abnormal Sides made those incredible push rod collars, and our Split-Fin rocker cover gave it the look, while our Finned Air-filter with K&N give it the air.

'Dog House Racing is Taiwan's premium exhaust fabricator. I have known him for years and always want to work with him, it's just our full black vintage-ish bikes don't fit with the Titanium rainbow he created. Now for this performance-driven bike it was the perfect chance to make a full titanium system, so we sat down together and came up with this design similar to our classic Bomber 2-into-1 pipe, but without heat shield and showing off the super nice pie-cut bents, and a full ti-tail section giving it the aggressive sound. Finally, I ordered full aluminium swing arm from Roaring Toyz and BDL open belt drive to give it a final weight shaving.

'After all these things I still go back to styling, made a narrow tank and raised super bike-ish tail section for that racy look. CT-garage helped with carb conversion, and final assembly, and as usual Air Runner Custom Paint finished it up with the nice factory grey just turned semi-glossy for a more aggressive look, which also helped tie in the beautiful rainbow colour the exhaust pipe made.'

Engine and carburettor detail of Graphite Speedster.

Year/Model: 2014

Engine Make/Size: HD/Rough Crafts dual front head 1584cc

Frame Make/Type: Rough Crafts billet/tubing

Front End Make/Type: Rough Crafts billet/tubing/ air springer

Rear suspension: Rough Crafts/Gears Racing in-frame shock

Rake: 29 degree

Stretch: None

Swingarm: Rough Crafts billet/tubing

Transmission/Drives/Clutch: Rough Crafts/BDL

Wheels F: RSD Diesel 3.50 × 18in

Wheels R: RSD Diesel 5.00 × 16in

Tyres F: Firestone dirt track ribbed 5.00 × 18in

Tyres R: Firestone dirt track ribbed 5.00 × 16in

Brakes F: Beringer inboard brake

Brakes R: Beringer inboard brake/Rough Crafts sprocket mod

Painter: Air Runner Custom Paint

Foot controls: Rough Crafts one-off mid

Handlebar controls: Rough Crafts/Performance Machine

Headlight: Rough Crafts grille-type headlight

Taillight: Rough Crafts grille-type LED taillight

Seat: Rough Crafts

Gas caps: Rough Crafts

Grips: Rough Crafts

Additional Info: The bike is based on vintage lines, with all modern tech. The look was going for a vintage rigid/springer bike but made with modern CNC billet/tubing bolted together softail with underseat rear shock and billet rear leg/tubing front leg springer with air shocks, quick release half tanks; left for electric inspection (battery and fuse), right side for fuel. Front and rear Beringer inboard brake rear modified with a sprocket makes a vintage drum brake look. Dual front S&S heads with dual FCR carbs, Rough Crafts custom-made billet lifter blocks. Push rod collars and head badge by 2 Abnormal Sides.

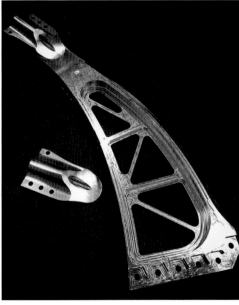

Opposite: **One beautiful engine coming together.**

Above left: **It's boring work but the finished results speak for themselves.**

Above: **Carburettors ready to be fitted.**

Left: **Machined aluminium billet form the backbone of the bike.**

Clockwise from left:

Is this a work of art?

The beautiful spine/backbone that also firms the shape of the fuel tank.

A glittering array of polished aluminium, gold and painted surfaces.

The electrical compartment is also formed by the curved spine.

Hooligan Tactics – Build Notes, by Winston Yeh

'After the Urban Cavalry build, the idea of a Sportster/Street Fighter version has always been on my mind.

'When an owner brought us a slightly modified 48, and told me to do whatever I wanted with it, that was the perfect chance. And it just so happened that I had an XR1200 turned vintage tracker build on the way; also it was perfect that I had an XR swingarm lying around for this build, plus the inverted forks, progressive piggyback shocks ... etc. It kind of just fell into place naturally. Then I developed a prototype seat/tail section that was about to go into production soon, and you'll see, it works out well with streetfighter, tracker, or café racer, which also will be demonstrated on our XR tracker build coming next. For the paintwork I wanted to push the "tactics" feel more, so I decided to go with a blue-ish grey digital camo that was rarely used in the custom Harley scene, and it worked out perfectly.'

With this bike I thought I would start with the close-ups and conclude with the finished bike:

Left: **Close-up of the V twins, matt black exhausts, and RC air filter.**

Right above: **RC seat.**

Right: **Progressive gas adjustable suspension and adjustable spring pressure.**

Year/Model: 2012 Sportster 48
Engine Make/Size: HD/1200
Frame Make/Type: HD/stock with slight modification
Front End Make/Type: Rough Crafts/Suzuki GSR-R600 inverted forks
Rear Shocks: Progressive Suspension 970 series shocks
Rake: Stock
Stretch: None
Trail: Stock
Swingarm: XR1200
Transmission/Drives/Clutch: Rough Crafts groove clutch cover
Exhausts: Rough Crafts Guerilla Exhausts
Wheels F: Arlen Ness Motorcycles 10 Gauge Wheel/18 × 3.50in
Wheels R: Arlen Ness Motorcycles 10 Gauge Wheel/17 × 6.25in
Tyre F: Dunlop £\-13Z 150/70ZR18
Tyre R: Dunlop £\-13Z 190/55ZR17
Brakes F: Performance Machine radial caliper/Lyndall racing brake composite rotors
Brakes R: Performance Machine radial caliper/Lyndall racing brake composite rotors/Kraus Moto Co. radial caliper mount
Painter: Air Runner Custom Paint
Chroming/Plating: Anodising
Assembly: CT-Garage
Foot controls: Stock Mids/Rough Crafts
Handlebars: Rough Crafts drag bars
Handlebar controls: Performance Machine/Rough Crafts
Headlight: Rough Crafts grille-type headlight

Turn signals/Taillight: Rough Crafts grille-type

Seat/Tail Section: Rough Crafts

Gas caps: Rough Crafts

Risers: Rough Crafts

Grips: Rough Crafts

RockerArm Cover: Rough Crafts Bomber XL rocker cover

Intake: Rough Crafts fin air filter

Clockwise from opposite top:
Simple black satin handlebars.

Digital effect camouflage paintwork RC gas cap. Feast your eyes on the black finish of the frame and steering head.

The advertising blurb says it all, and is part of the finished paintwork. You could say it's a rolling advertisement.

Dinky little grilled brake light, or is it a turn indicator?

RC gear cover, foot pegs and brake pedal. Exposed final drive.

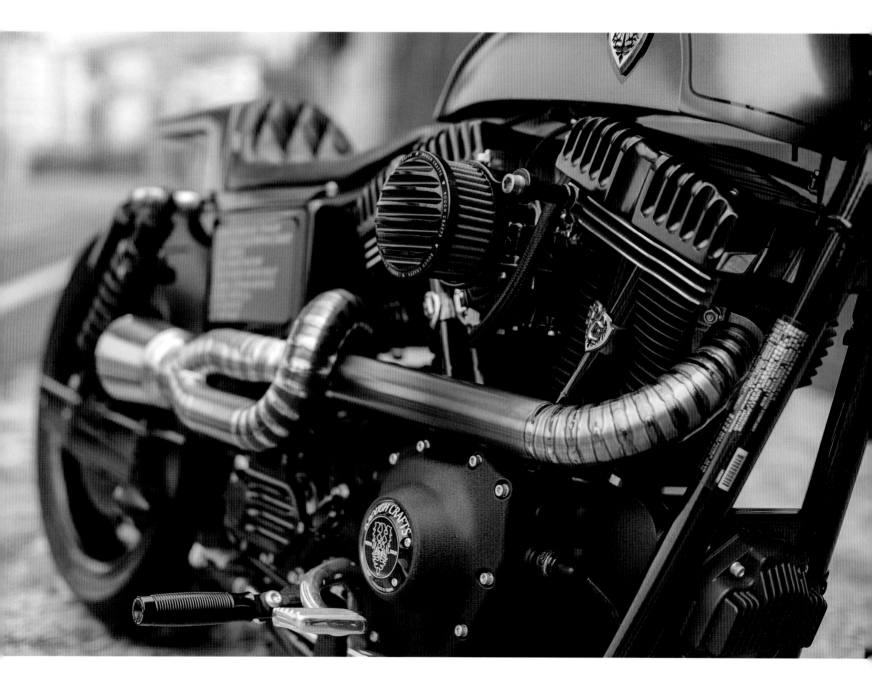

Rusty Slider – Build Notes

Winston tells the story:

'This build started with a three-way collaboration between two of my friends' brands, Taki Design and Provider Production, and the giant of work wear, Dickies.

'The whole collaboration is tied in with the biker and worker style of clothing. At one of our regular meetings, the idea of Rough Crafts building a bike project to tie in the two companies seemed a good idea, especially if Dickies had a donor bike. Fortunately it turned out that Dickies Taiwan's owner has an XR1200, and had just been through a small crash a few days before, so it was perfect timing. The XR1200 is actually a good bike but the stock design aesthetic is just wrong in a lot of ways. However, the tracker-style bike is always one of the directions we're always interested to go with, and the old XR750 racer is just simply one of the coolest bikes ever. So the direction was clear: turn a 2010 XR1200 in to an XR750-style street tracker.

'The build was actually almost side-by-side with our Hooligan Tactics, so we took the forty-eight stock front forks and swingarm from the vintage tracker look. The stock XR has an upward EFI system, which is a headache for us. There is all that complex fuel injection stuff, which is certainly not attractive, so we changed it to a Mikuni HSR42 carb going on side to run our Velocity Stacks. Shaping the style, it's a Sportster tank stretched by almost 2in and cut thinner for the slick side profile. The seat/tail section is the same as on Hooligan Tactics, which is our production prototype.

'For the exhausts, the SuperTrapp 2 into 2 tracker pipe has always had a place in my heart. So when one of my friends was selling his a couple of years ago, I couldn't help myself buying it, for no reason and with no idea of what to do with it, but now the perfect opportunity had arrived. But I couldn't see a way to bolt it on directly, so I massaged the header of the rear cylinder to turn and fit into the front header, made another long megaphone and billet end cap, and there it is, a one-off Rough Crafts 2 into 1 tracker pipe. The other details you can pretty much see on the tech sheet. For the paint, to match Dickies' workwear without making it a "theme" bike, I asked Air Runner Custom Paint to do a slightly rusted bare metal trick paint, and this is what he delivered. Yes, trust me, it's amazing – and it's all paint.'

Rusty slider – and no, it's not a rusty bike by the seashore, it's a very clever and skilful bit of paintwork.

Year/Model: 2010 XR1200

Engine Make/Size: HD/1200

Frame Make/Type: HD/stock with slight modification

Front End Make/Type: Rough Crafts trees/HD 48 forks black ti-coated

Rear Shocks: Progressive Suspension 970 series shocks

Rake: Stock

Stretch: None

Trail: Stock

Swingarm: HD 48

Transmission/Drives/Clutch: Rough Crafts groove clutch cover

Exhausts: Rough Crafts Tracker 2 into 1

Wheels F: Roland Sands Design Del Mar Wheel/ 19 × 3.00in

Wheels R: Roland Sands Design Del Mar Wheel/ 19 × 3.00in

Tyres F: Maxxis DTR-1 27.5 × 7.5-19

Tyres R: Maxxis DTR-1 27.5 × 7.5-19

Brakes F: Performance Machine 6-piston caliper/ Lyndall racing brake composite rotors

Brakes R: Performance Machine 4-piston caliper/ Lyndall racing brake composite rotors

Painter: Air Runner Custom Paint

Chroming/Plating: Anodising

Assembly: CT-Garage

Foot controls: Roland Sands Design Mids/ISR master cylinder/Rough Crafts

Handlebars: Rough Crafts fighter bars

Handlebar controls: Performance Machine/Rough Crafts

Headlight: Rough Crafts grille-type headlight

Indicators/Taillight: Rough Crafts grille-type

Seat/Tail Section: Rough Crafts

Gas caps: Rough Crafts

Risers: Rough Crafts

Grips: Rough Crafts

Intake: Rough Crafts Fin Velocity Stacks/Mikuni HSR42 carb conversion

Rough Crafts clutch cover & Roland Sands design footpegs.

Clockwise from left:
Fancy a blast along an empty beach – maybe in your dreams?

The connection with Dickies workwear is unmistakable.

The imitation rustwork is amazing.

Mikuni carbs, RC intake. Fabulous use of satin and matt black finishing.

Slate Hammer – Build Notes

How did this bike come to be? Winston tells the story:

'This bike was commissioned by a very good friend of mine who owns the clothing brand Taki (www. facebook.com/taki.design).

'He was never really into bikes before, but now he likes to travel with us. Custom bikes grew on him very fast, and this year his brand had a series of biker-influenced themes called The Road Leader, and because he couldn't resist the desire to have a custom any longer, he had to have one, so naturally he came to me. He wanted a café racer, he wanted it clean and a grey-ish colour; that's pretty much the whole brief. Fortunately, I had known him for years and you get a sense of what a guy really wants, so the ideas for his ideal bike came thick and fast.

'The key component is the vintage replica Dunstall GT half fairing by GFTP (www.caferacingparts. com). It looks perfect for sizing, but the vintage windscreen was too high for the slick look I'm after, so I heated the screen and tilted it way lower. For the tank, it was actually a super heavily modified HD Sportster tank, the Rough Crafts signature cut from the centre perfectly created that café tank look. The interesting wider front wrapped around the front cylinder head, while the rear was narrowed and cut out to accommodate the rear cylinder head, which is one of the most interesting shapes I created for this particular bike.

'Now to the matching tail section. I wanted the clean lightweight look of the empty mid-space, so an under-tail oil tank was made. The custom RCE lithium battery was tucked in under the gas tank, and the stainless steel belly pan was only for ECM and fuse, etc. The Speed Merchant (www. thespeedmerchant.net) provided the riser-less billet triple tree, lower legs from an 883R. For the dual-caliper mounts, a pair of Brembo-made HD Touring calipers, San Diego Customs (www. sandiegocustoms.com) and Lyndall Racing Brakes (www.lyndallbrakes.com) teamed up with this Speedline wheel/discs/pulley set wrapped with Firestone Deluxe Champion tyres. The rear was Progressive Suspension 15in shocks. Our very good friends Back Drop Custom Leather (www.back-drop. com) from Japan wrapped that beautiful seat for us; Spark (www.spark.it) provided us the tail pipe, and we made a full stainless header to run it. Rearsets were custom made, the custom full silver push rod collars were again made by our talented friend from 2 Abnormal Sides (www.2abnormalsides.com) and, of course, the paint was handled by none other than Air Runner Custom Paint Studio (www.facebook. com/airrunner.C.P).

'The bike actually has nothing to do with Aston Martin, but when I was planning for the photo shoot, Aston Martin Taiwan called me and said it wanted an interview with me in its magazine for their VIPs. I thought it would be a cool idea to shoot the bike in the Aston Martin show room with one of their cars.

Photos by Bobby Ho.

Slate hammer – bike or Aston Martin? I can't make up my mind.

Clockwise from left:

I just love those decorative push rod tubes.

The seat detail is exquisite workmanship.

Where does all the 'gubbins' go? Under the seat, of course.

SINROJA

When I first contacted Rahul Sinroja via email I thought impulsively and erroneously that he lived and worked somewhere exotic like Calcutta or Delhi, but no, when I eventually got his address, it was Leicester. Oh well, you live and learn. Here Rahul tells his story:

'I was born and brought up in a rather small town in India, where bikes are something of a daily requirement. No one thinks of it as a hobby or form of joy, merely a transport, which is quite sad. Yet for me it was always something more exciting, something that made me smile every time I heard an engine. I was probably 10-years-old when I first sneaked out on my brother's bike (hero Honda Splendor) which was our sort of first custom with wire wheels, changed to alloys, decals stripped and replaced with custom decals and full silver paint job. I guess this is where it all really started. We didn't have lot of fancy bikes in India back then but the ding, ding rumble of a 2-stroke Yamaha RX100 or the thump of a Royal Enfield Bullet would always get my heart racing.

'Along with bikes, my interest in machines in general grew with time. My family had owned manufacturing businesses for generations, making moulds for shoe soles, and designing and manufacturing injection-moulded plastic toys.

Growing up, I always got excited with machines in my dad's factory, and that is where, for the first time, I got my hands on a lathe along with my brother. We wanted to buy some exercise weights but our father said: "We own a factory in which you can let your brains go wild with imagination and, even better, we have machines to make anything you want, so why not make those weights." Well, we did the exact thing; turned some nice dumbbells for us and the little engineer in me was brought to life. The bodybuilder died rather quickly.

'Fast forward a few years, when I turned 16, I moved to England with my family and then got carried away in the cultural routines of education, work experiences and jobs to boost my CV. I then decided to start a university degree in mechanical engineering with this growing fascination of machines and loved every bit of it. We learned everything from the very basics of engineering and setting up a business to breaking down a brand new DB9 (yes we actually shredded a DB9 into pieces for the purpose of learning (I cried a little) and how things should be put together.

'Whilst at university I followed this new wave custom culture whilst learning all things engineering and business. My interest in opening an engineering-related business grew, and what

The R1.

better than motorbikes? So I started looking out for more and more ways of doing it. I visited shows, read magazines, online blogs, the whole thing. Then I came across Bike Shed London last year, and I decided to visit it. I shall be honest, since childhood I've been in love with bikes, cars and machines, but Bike Shed London changed everything; I loved the show, the scene, the people and the bikes. I decided to do something about this growing passion of mine. I saved some money from my weekend job of selling phones and bought a BMW R80. I just love these boxers, the engine has so much character, and a lot of parts can be bolted on easily to make it better, and I can engineer the rest. Until then I wasn't allowed to get a motorbike, as my family always feared the worst, as they all do. Yes, I didn't even have a licence until I almost finished my first build.

'I started a full-time job after university as an engineer to save some funds. After I spent a few more months at my daily job, I secured a loan to fund the business and the first build. Then came 3 January 2015, and I decided to start my business on the same day as my 24th birthday (yeah it's a bit cheesy but it was sort of a present for myself, and started me on my dream vocation). I set the Kickback Custom competition in March as a deadline for my build as I knew coming somewhere in the top three would give me some good press and get my business out there. So I cleaned up the shed, made a wooden ramp and started the pursuit of happiness (cliché but true).'

The R1 Donor Bike: Model: BMW R80 RT Monolever, 1989

'The idea behind the design was to create a simple and clean bike,' explains Rahul. 'Smooth lines flowing along the bike, no cluttered cables nothing, yet keeping it as original as possible and giving that factory look as if this is how it was supposed to be – and it wouldn't work otherwise. Use high quality parts, replace as many moving parts as possible to give it a genuinely new life, and finally have a high-quality finish and attention to detail.

'From here the whole strip down started. Luckily I'd been planning this whole build for a while so things moved swiftly. I have made a few key business contacts within the industry to help me with my builds. It helps speed up the build and also brings a wealth of experience into every build, which all our customers appreciate. People including Steve at SED, Towza at Towzatronics and Glen at GD design are the best in the business in what they do, which enables me to ensure all the work is done to the highest standard available. This well-set system enables us to turn around bikes at a good pace, with better quality and at affordable prices.

'Every single thing on the bike was taken apart. Even though it was well taken care of, it needed a new lease of life. The frame was de-tabbed before going for a sand blast along with wheels, swing-arm, stands, triples and lower forks. Then it got gloss black spray paint rather than typical powder coat to get a high-quality finish and it's easier to repair chips with paint (all our customers get touch

up paint with their bikes so they don't have to waste trips down to us for little chip repairs or pay anyone to do little things).

'After the full strip down of the bike, the engine, carbs, gearbox, bevel and clutch got a media blast treatment, new replacements parts such as bearings and gaskets and then a rebuild by Steve under our request. During the process all these parts got a layer of satin paint and I hand-sanded the fins to just highlight the lines on the bike but still show the black paint in the rough surface to highlight the casting process that was used in manufacturing these parts thirty-odd years before.

'When the engine got all its horses back and the carbs were fine-tuned, it got married back to the frame. The wheels went on with new Dunlop StreetSmart rubbers for perfect all-weather grip and good speed rating so the horses can be put to use. We used Hagen customised shocks for the bike's new weight and riding requirements, whilst lowering it by 10mm for better stance, and the front fork springs were upgraded to new progressive springs (bike rides and handles superbly now). Vonzetti provided the subframe (I'm not the best welder yet) and seat to match our requirements along with the airbox and Monza cap to complete the visual needs of this bike. Motogadget, being undoubtedly one of the best gadget makers, was chosen for its tiny speedo and keyless ignition (it still overwhelms a lot of people) to match the elegant and simple design of the bike.

'The paint scheme was chosen to give the bike a modern feel with old school signature BMW pinstripes on the tank. The looping structures of the bike such as the top loop on the tank, frame and wheels were all painted gloss black, whereas the sides/perpendicular items including the engine and sides of the tank were painted satin to make the lines of the bike flow better. Finally, to balance the brown diamond stitched seat, the forks were covered with the same material (stitched by my mum – not the seat, just the fork covers) and brown grips were added and a special little touch around the Monza cap. Renthal low bars and standard (but refurbished and painted) controls completed the steering. Under the tank the brand new reconfigured electronics (thanks to Towza) lives with the battery neatly hidden under the seat.

'Since I completed the bike we have been so overwhelmed with the response we received from the public. I never expected my business to get rolling just off one bike. Since the very first day when we displayed it at Kickback Custom bike show everyone loved my attention to detail and quality of finish and the fact that the bike looks like as if it was meant to be like that. Nothing over the top, nothing massively different to what many people have done, but I've gone above and beyond with little things which has paid off and makes it stand out. Following the Kickback show came the real deal, the dream place that made all this happen this quick in first place, The Bike Shed London. We got a great response there, in fact, we got a commission build straight on the spot as the customer couldn't get his eye off it. And later on Sunday evening, Ross

and Vicky brought us to meet a potential client and my brother and I secured two more commissions. Our Facebook page shot off the roof, going from 200-odd likes to over 1,000.

'We are now about to finish R2 and R3 commission builds, and looking forward to building three more in line over the winter for the next Bike Shed London (hopefully Paris too) and the season of shows. We are also taking commissions to work on over the winter so our customers can have a chance to ride as soon the first sun is out (only a few slots left). We are also developing parts and kits for our clients who want to take on the building challenge themselves. Alongside all this we are also providing powder coating, tank painting and a BMW engine rebuild service. All this will be on the website soon (I'm not great at making websites yet either so I am learning as we go).

'Even though we absolutely loved that bike, and I know there will never be another first, sadly we decided to put it up for sale. Until now we have had people interested but were not sure what to do, but in order to get the business going we don't seem to have a choice. We are entertaining offers now and realise that customer satisfaction is a must for us, and hence the bike comes with a comprehensive one-year electrical and mechanical warranty and three years of free servicing. This also shows our interest in building long-term relationships with clients. Lastly, we also want to know how our bikes are doing and if there are certain issues that we can improve on in future builds.'

Mechanical Spec

Full ground up nut-and-bolt rebuild of the engine. Basically it is a zero-hour engine now, given back all of its lost horses. All seals, inlet outlet valves, piston rings, gaskets, etc. were replaced with new better-performing parts. Everything was aqua blasted and inspected before painting them black with special engine paint. Thanks to Scriminger Engine Developments. The carbs stripped, sonic cleaned and assembled with new jets, diaphragms, gaskets, etc. The bevel drive was stripped clean, blasted and painted, then assembled with new bearings.

Head(s): Standard.

Barrel Pistons: Standard.

Cams: Standard.

Carburettors/fuel injection: 32mm constant depression bing carbs.

Airbox/filters: K&N performance oval filters.

Crank: Standard.

Clutch: Dry single plate.

Gearbox: 5-speed gearbox.

Ignition system: Bosch contact-free electronic ignition.

Exhaust: Keihan SS downpipes with megaphone mufflers.

Power Output: Approx. 50–60hp.

Frame: Mainframe like all other parts was sandblasted and de-tabbed and painted with show quality gloss black paint and lacquered for extra gloss finish. Subframe was replaced with a matching 1in tubing frame for a clean and even look from Vonzetti made to our requirement. Battery box fabricated and moved under the seat. Rear footrests were removed as it's a single seater ideally (who needs a third wheel, right?) and fronts are standard footrest but they were sandblasted and painted then covered with new rubbers.

Front End

Forks: The front forks were overhauled with new seals and new Hagon progressive springs. Blasted and painted.

Yokes: Yokes were blasted and painted with new head bearings. They were modified to accommodate new custom-made headlight bracket.

Wheel: 18in standard BMW wheels stripped and painted with Dunlop StreetSmart tyres good for all weather riding not purely for the show.

Discs: 285mm BMW twin discs.

Calipers: Brembo 2-piston caliper.

Brake lines: Brand new custom Venhill brake lines.

Handlebars: Renthal low handlebars.

Master Cylinders: BMW standard cylinder overhauled with new seals and painted black to match the rest of the bike.

Switchgear: Standard but again taken apart and overhauled and restored with new bearings and seals.

Clocks: Motogadget MST Speedster tiny speedo.

Rear End

Swinging arm: BMW Monolever swinging arm with new bearings

Shock(s): Hagon custom shock made to match this bike and rider's specification

Wheel: Standard 18in wheel blasted and painted black with Dunlop StreetSmart tyres

Brake: BMW standard drum brakes at rear with new shoes and springs

Drive
Shaft Driven: Fully overhauled shaft

Bodywork
Front Mudguard: Taken off, as who needs clutter?
Fairing: Taken off
Petrol Tank: Stripped, sealed and press treated from inside and show quality two-tone paint job with subtle metallic gloss with matt on side to enhance the BMW logo and match the engine's matt finish. Paint by GD.
Design Seat: Custom-made diamond stitch leather finish seat (from Vonzetti).
Tailpiece/Rear Guard: Custom-made to hold the rear light and number plate.

Electrics
Main Loom: Brand new electrics fully redone using heavy-duty wires with multiple fuses for ease of fault finding. BMW originally just came with two fuses in whole system, which generally isn't reliable enough. Thanks to Towzatronics for their great help.
Ignition switch: Wireless Gear's Racing in-frame shock ignition system.
Headlight: Aftermarket Halo headlight with signature BMW LED angel eye.
Tail Light: LED Bates taillight.
Indicators: Billet machined aluminium LED indicators.

Paint Scheme
Colour(s): The whole bike was designed on dark/black tone with subtle differences in the finish. E.g. the tank has matt and gloss finish with fine metal flakes that only shines through when lights hit

the tank. Then the two finishes were separated by signature BMW Pinstripe loop.

'There were a lot of influences on this build,' adds Rahul. 'For years I have followed many bike builders around the world such as Down and Out Café Racer, Hazan Motorworks, Shinya Kimura, Café Racer Dreams, Debolex Engineering, etc. via website and magazines/forums including The Bike Shed, 100% Biker, BSH, Bike Exif, etc.

'Even though it's my own work, design and idea, this bike inevitably has influences from all those mentioned. I would take this opportunity to thank them all and many others for being an inspiration or source of it. Along with special thanks to my brother for always being there for me.'

The R3 story: BMW R100 R Monolever, 1993

'This one is a special build for us as we tried to push our skill set and design possibilities,' says Rahul.

'The story of the bike started at Bike Shed London 2015 where we displayed our first bike, the R1. We got to talking to a young man called James who couldn't contain his excitement after seeing the bike. We saw James and his friend come around the bike a few times throughout the day before he approached us and just said, "Guys I love this bike and can't keep my eyes off it, I've not seen this attention to detail on any other BMW and I want you to build me a bike!" The moment he said that, I knew it had paid off taking that leap, quitting the job and spending all the money I could borrow from the bank. We got to chatting with James and it soon became clear that this bike was going to be something totally different than what we had done, and it was going to challenge us a lot along the way. The hurdles we jumped were just not bike-related, the timeline of the build got hammered when our beloved neighbours complained about us doing business from home. Then the council banned us from building bikes, after which we almost lost more than two months of build time before we found a new workshop and settled in.

'We found a nice ex-police BMW R80 that had spoked wheels, as that was a big requirement as everything else could be replaced without adding crazy costs. We stripped the bike and during that time we had a few more meetings with James and decided we wanted to change the donor bike. He preferred 1000cc in hindsight, so we then made sure he got what he wanted. So after six or so weeks into the build we decided to change the donor bike as it was too expensive to change big end kits and carbs. So we were back to square one, but then my friend came in to rescue us and sold us his R100R. This meant we could fit even bigger tyres without much modification, have wired wheels, a 1000cc engine and carb set-up and a monoshock, which he then preferred, too. From this point on, the build finally got under way and we confirmed that there were no more changes to be made in terms of replacing the donor bike. Both parties were happy with this new bike and we got cracking.

'As with all our bikes, they all get proper Sinroja treatment, which means a full engine, gearbox and carbs strip down (Scriminger Engine Developments were brought in again but this time we did them in house under Steve's guidance, so from now on we do all engine, gearbox and carb rebuilds in-house). All the electronics were binned too and replaced with brand new wiring by Towza at Towzatronics with the aid of the highly reliable m-Unit and the whole set of Motogadget accessories including the front and rear indicators, speedo, grips, m-Switches and RFID ignition. The wheels to hold the mighty Coker Beck tyres were custom-made with both 16in stainless rims and spokes thanks to Hagon. Now the beast had a good grip! (Not the best tyres in the wet though.)

'While the strip down/mocking up was going on, I came across a set of Yamaha R1 upside down front end forks on eBay (scouring eBay is part of a builder's life!), which I thought would be cool on a future café racer project I had in mind for myself. (I doubt I'll ever get time to build my own bike). So I went ahead, picked it up and as I walked into the garage with the front end in my hand I saw the R3 with its original front end looking great but still not perfect. 'Mean' is the word James used in his first sentence to me and the bike was still missing something to be mean-looking. That was it, I realised straight away that this front end had to go on the bike (the exact reason why my bike will never be built; everything I buy for it goes to customers). I did a quick mock-up and it was a winner. I quickly took a picture, sent it to James and he couldn't agree more. We both knew it had to be done. Thanks to James as he agreed to fork out some more of his hard-earned cash for a new front end.

'Next, I was on the way to Danny at Fastec Custom Racing for bespoke machining. After going through some designs and ideas we had a custom front end with brand new yokes, lasered with our name, recessed to accommodate Motogadget speedo and warning lights. The forks were fully overhauled and anodised black to go with the dark theme of the bike. The stopping power was provided with two wavy EBC performance brakes held on by machined spacers that are a work of art behind the scenes (see if you can spot them through the disc).

'The next thing we were on to was the exhaust system. We had already binned the idea of using

standard downpipes on this build. We wanted something special, and I've always loved the idea of the pipes running under the seat. It just gives a bike lovely lines, makes it a lot meaner and says "performance". So that's what we did, we got them made in stainless steel, and then gave it a brushed effect to match the polished fins on the engine and balance the lines of the bike. My OCD resulted in mufflers matching the exact curvature of the subframe at the back just to finish them off nicely. They sound the business and look even better.

'The bike also has a lot of little details such as: the hubs were painted and we had its fins polished, the fuel cap was machined out of billet aluminium and holds our logo, Hayabusa controls, the stripes on the tank that are metallic gloss black compared to the flat blue that sparkles under lights. The rear passenger rests are machined and removable, depending on whether James plans to carry a passenger or not. The gear lever was cheap sheet metal so we replaced it with a custom billet-machined lever, the rear twin lights reflect the lines from headlight and tank and kind of finishes off the bike, while the rear indicators curve perfectly around the mufflers. The number plate mount that comes around at the back of the tyre braces with a steel mesh that also covers the battery box, keeping consistency in the design. This bike has really helped us learn a lot, and also helped us see outside the box, which is essential in this business. Everyone loved the bike at the show, including James, whom we promised 'a ride of a lifetime, every time'.

'From just being a weekend bike, it has become a regular commuter for James as he can't keep his hands off it, which makes us feel really proud of our work. The business is looking positive now that we have already grown our new workshop. The bike count is on R7 and books are full until October. We are now taking bookings for winter projects for clients looking to ride next summer. We have some great bikes in the pipeline including two Honda café racer projects. They'll be kitted with some great kit including race cams, high-compression pistons, CR carbs, GSXR front end, and new rear suspension geometry. These projects will help us show our skill set outside the BMW market and show that we can just about make anything cooler. We will also be launching our online shop soon with some bespoke parts and accessories for the custom industry.'

Opposite top: **What a gorgeous, minimalist instrument panel.**

The Sinroja brothers certainly love their BMWs.

Model: BMW R100 R Monolever, 1993

Mechanicals: Full ground up nut and bolt rebuild of the engine. Basically it is a zero-hour engine now, giving back all its lost horses. All the seals, inlet outlet valves, piston rings, gaskets, etc. were replaced with new better-performing parts. Everything was aqua blasted and inspected before painting them black with special engine paint. Thanks to Scriminger Engine Developments. The carbs were stripped, sonic cleaned and assembled with new jets, diaphragms, gaskets, etc. The bevel drive was stripped clean, blasted and painted, then assembled with new bearings.

Head(s): Standard

Barrel Pistons: Standard

Cams: Standard

Carburettors/fuel injection: 40mm constant depression bing carbs

Airbox/filters: K&N performance oval filters

Crank: Standard

Clutch: Dry single plate

Gearbox: 5-speed gearbox

Ignition system: Bosch contact-free electronic ignition

Exhaust: Custom stainless exhaust thanks to Zorstec

Power Output: Approx. 50–60hp

Frame: Mainframe like all other parts was sandblasted and de-tabbed, and powder-coated subframe was replaced with a matching 1in tubing frame for a clean and even look custom-made for the bike and its requirements. Battery box fabricated and moved under the seat. Footrests have lost their rubbers and now just powder-coated with removable rear foot rests.

Front End

Forks: Taken from Yamaha R1, fully stripped and rebuilt in black with new stanchions

Yokes: Custom-made from billet aluminium that holds the speedo and warning lights with company name engraved in front

Wheel: 16in custom rims and Coker Beck tyres

Discs: EBC performance discs fastened on to bespoke machined spacers

Calipers: 2-piston caliper off Yamaha R1

Brake lines: Brand new custom Venhill brake lines

Handlebars: Billet machined by Fastec Racing to match the bike

Master Cylinders: Nissin master cylinder off GSXR 1000

Switchgear: Motogadget Mini switches to keep the cockpit clean and tidy

Clocks: Motogadget mini speedo with warning lights

Rear End

Swinging arm: BMW Paralever swinging arm with new bearings

Shock(s): Hagon custom shock made to match this bike and rider's specification

Wheels: Custom 16in rims and Coker Beck tyres

Brakes: BMW Standard Drum brakes at rear with new shoes and springs

Drive

Shaft Driven: Fully overhauled shaft

Bodywork

Front Mudguard: Taken off

Fairing: Taken off

Petrol Tank: Stripped, sealed and pressure treated from inside, and shows quality paint job in flat baby blue with gloss metallic black lines to enhance the BMW logo and match the engine's matt finish

Paint: GD Design

Seat: Custom-made leather seat from Glenn Moger

Electrics

Main Loom: Brand new electrics fully redone using heavy duty cables and reliable Motogadget m-Unit. Thanks to Towzatronics.

Ignition switch: Wireless Motogadget ignition system

Headlight: Aftermarket headlight with machined grille

Tail Light: LED tail light in custom housing

Indicators: Motogadget bar ends in front and pins in rear

Photo credits: Photography & post-production Ivo Ivanov. Technical and photography assistant Evgeni Chipev.

TRICANA

I have two of Jonathan Natario's rather wonderful creations for you to feast your eyes on for the next few pages: his truly beautiful Mondego, based around a Moto Guzzi frame and motor, and a Triumph – two very different motorcycles, as I am sure you will agree. However, not only are they simply gorgeous, sumptuous and delectable machines – I am running out of superlatives again – they are the most stunning photographs. And it's at this juncture that I take my hat off and pay silent homage to the photographers, and the important part that they play with their own particular skills in making the most of these very special bikes. Enjoy, but be very afraid because as soon as you have seen them you may very well want to rush out and order one. I wonder if as a writer I could get a free sample? Nah.

Jonathan started the Tricana Custom Bike Building business in 2011, not long after finishing a brown Moto Guzzi (the 750 café). He bought that bike in London back in 2009, while he was doing his MSc in Motorsport Engineering at Oxford Brooks University. Back then, bike building at Tricana was a small affair, but the only regular work that he had. In 2011–13 he built the Guzzi 750 Café, Mondego, Briosa, Saudade, and a very nice project with a Suzuki DR Big 800 for long off-road distances.

After that, he decided to move to Switzerland and, of course, he had to put Tricana on pause for a while, so the business's future was not very clear. He then started

It is a wondrous object.

to work in Switzerland as a motorcycle mechanic in a Harley-Davidson garage, then at the end of 2015 he had the opportunity to restart Tricana Motorcycles with an MV Agusta dealer. Things were looking up. Since then he has rented a garage that had been a Ducati dealership for at least thirty years, so it made perfect sense to start to repair Ducatis since he had all the equipment. Jonathan progressed from that and is now also an Aprilia dealer, not bad eh? Of course, he does all he can to keep up with the custom building scene around the world, but he has to earn his bread and butter with the bike repair work, and then find spare time to work on his own designs and builds.

Opposite top left: **The seat of desire.**

Opposite top right: **Glossy green paintwork with gold pinstripes, shapely gas taps and deliciously designed leather restraining strap.**

Above: **Foot controls and clean centre section.**

Left: **Twin leading show (TLS) front brake.**

Right: **Has a Moto Guzzi ever looked this good?**

Opposite top: **Tricana 1, the Bonneville café racer.**

Opposite left: **I'm not too sure about the dropped handlebars myself, but stylish they certainly are.**

Opposite right: **The stitched leatherwork on the tank and seat is meticulous.**

Right: **With Jonathan on board.**

MARTYN WILKINS

UK

Now, as they say, for something completely different. The next two bikes have been built by a talented young man named Martyn Wilkins who only lives some 20 miles from me, and over the last six months I have got to know him quite well. He was trained in engineering and for some years worked at Warwick University, so he knows a few things about working with materials, especially metals.

Martyn's introduction to bike restoration started many years ago when he and his dad worked on an old BSA Sunbeam scooter from 1963. Sometime later this would be the impetus for the CB450 project completed in 2015. When I asked him what motivates a biker to take on such a daunting project, he answers that it's a combination of many complex feelings. Watching Café Racer TV for inspiration helped to focus on what was already being produced on the custom scene by such worthies as Australians Deus Ex Machina *et al.*, but it's really the desire to create and ride a bike that no one else has.

The BSA had been a project to restore what was original, but in the end Martyn found that process very restrictive. However, a purely custom project would allow him to use his creative and engineering skills to the limit. Deep in many a biker's psyche lies the feeling that the 1960s and '70s were the glory days of motorcycling. This was no doubt influenced by a new era where young people had that new thing – disposable income! And

they were going to use it in the pursuit of style and freedom. And so the Honda CB450 was chosen because the concept was to produce something that in general style was similar to the old 1960s British café racers, with a twin engine and typical tubular frame, and indeed the CB450 was initially introduced in 1965, becoming later labelled The Black Bomber. It was an advanced bike for its day but not totally appreciated at the time, and it never realised the sales that Honda hoped for. In the UK in 1965, it sold for £360, about the same price as a British 650, but it was far more sophisticated.

For an engine designed in 1963, having double overhead cams and utilising torsion bars for valve control, it was indeed cutting edge. Add to that the progressive and more practical use of a 12v system

Opposite: **Honda CB450 at the end of the journey.**

Above: **The 'Black Bomber' at the start of the journey.**

Work starts on the engine.

powering an electric start, it certainly outclassed the mid-1960s competition, on paper at any rate. Unfortunately as a complete package, the whole style of the bike was unattractive. On the other side of the coin, the CB450 does possess a rather good-looking engine, and with the benefit of the designer's 'eye' Martin could see it being the focal point of his own project.

So the engine, the frame and the hubs were the essentials to hang on to, as for pretty much everything else, well that had to go – on eBay, where else? The first thing to do was to strip the bike entirely, this then enabled him to work on the frame and the engine, whilst researching parts online and designing other features that would be purely personal and innovative. The frame was de-lugged and cleaned up, while a tubular semicircular frame section to act as the seat support needed to be designed. Once the dimensions for this were finalised, the drawings went to One Off

Engineering, which made an excellent job of the part. Modifications to the frame included adding an extended swing arm from a Honda CB360, which would provide a stretched café racer look. This meant that Martyn would later have to source and purchase totally different shock absorbers but the present ones would do for preliminary mock-ups. Later on Hagon was most helpful with advice, and supplied the longer shocks that were required. The frame needed strengthening in a couple of areas, and the photos show where Martyn had to design a couple of steel gussets to go between the seat tubes. Usually he makes a template out of cardboard (his tip of the month) and converts that to a DXF file before using computer aided design (CAD) to draw and cut the piece before welding into place. The alloy tank (£500) and seat (£200) both came from Legendary Motorcycles US, as did the headlight and bracket. The original hubs were taken to Central Wheels, which constructed both front and rear wheels, but there was some additional work to make the Suzuki SV650 front end and discs fit to the new wheel arrangement. The aluminium rims were powder-coated black by the same company.

Meanwhile, the engine was stripped, and having an engineering background was obviously helpful as one of the first jobs was to press apart the crank, place it on a lathe to lighten it and then dynamically balance it. These fundamental improvements simply make for a smoother and better engine, and Martyn did that job himself. The headstock came from a Suzuki SV650 and that required work to fill in unwanted holes, and then a classy red Honda badge was inserted for artistic effect. The downpipes are standard CB450, but the silencers are reverse cone megas – very noisy, but very period.

The wiring and ignition was going to be entirely new, and this was where you have to be your own research and development department. However, help was at hand in the shape of Motogadget, a high-class instrument and electronic accessory company based in Germany that uses cutting edge technology, quality and style for anyone making their own custom builds. This internet-accessed company supplied a whole host of parts to bring the bike bang up to date and also make it much more reliable. We have to add that these parts don't come cheap but they are high quality, and they included a whole host of coloured wiring, plus rev counter with inbuilt speedo, designed into one attractive unit. Then there were the indicators and their grips, and all the classy black and alloy switchgear. These products are not only stylish but work very well, and the decision was made to solder all the joints because snap connectors can prove to be troublesome as time goes on.

The aluminium seat base was the perfect place to lay out all the electrical components, as can be seen from the photos. The seat was upholstered by a local guy, Mark at Dragon Seating, a real craftsman. The old carbs weren't going to cut it so CR carburettors were sourced and purchased from Power Barn in the US. These are Keihin CR36 racing carbs, and certainly look the part. Once the crank was finished it was time to turn to the engine rebuild. The gearbox was fine, but the old pistons and con rods had had it, so Todd Henning high compression pistons from the US were fitted once the barrels had been rebored to 500cc; and casings, head and barrels were vapour blasted to get them cleaned

Above: **Beautiful custom controls.**

Left: **Electrics go under the custom seat.**

A transformed CB450, now a café racer.

up. Martyn also spent some time polishing the inlet and exhaust ports for improved gas flow. New cams came from Phil Joy of Joy Engineering, who uses his own cam geometry, working along with resurfaced cam followers.

Rob: So Martyn; did you enjoy the process and are you pleased with the result?

Martyn: Very, the bike has already won several prizes for looks and engineering. For me, the prizes aren't what it's about, but it is satisfying to have your work appreciated. Also, it's a fabulous ride, and surprisingly comfortable; and I enjoyed the build so much I am now on my next project.

Rob: And the cost?

Martyn: Parts were obviously expensive, and I guess that on the whole build, I spent around £7,000, so please don't tell the wife.

Suzuki GT750, Martyn's Second Build

If Leonard Nimoy were still alive he would say: 'It's a GT750 Jim, but not as we know it.' And he would be right, for this type of conversion is way beyond your average bike fettler's ability, being undertaken by two university engineers who are at pains to state that they are not professional motorcycle builders. Having said that, between the two of them they have a considerable amount of skill and knowledge. To indicate the gulf between a standard Kettle and Martyn's café racer, I have included a picture of the Standard K model that I owned back in the wild days of 1978. That bike was fabulous, and I have to say that it was light years ahead of the BSA A10 that I had just replaced it with. I loved to turn the ignition on the Suzuki just to watch all those pretty coloured lights come on, and then to simply press a button to fire up the engine, and not have to jump furiously up and down to get the motor going.

Rob: Martyn, this is your second foray into the world of café racers, so what did you learn from doing the first, and why choose the Suzuki GT750, a grand symbol of the bikes from the 1970s if ever there was one?
Martyn: Well I was so proud of the Honda 450 and the way it turned out, that I got hooked on designing and making my own bike. Yes I learned a lot from the first build, how to fit electronic systems and electronic ignition were two new fields, and that's before you have to start designing stylish brackets to fit your brakes and gear lever pedals to. But one thing you need to have is a database of what there is out there to draw from. Now this database could be on paper or on your computer, but

it's better to have the information running around in your head, i.e. who specialises in what, so that you can draw on their experience, and also the innumerable websites where you can buy the exact parts you require for your build. Take Jim Lomas for instance. He originated from the UK but now has a business specialising in making exhausts for two strokes including the GT750. Without that knowledge, you would be stuck with your stock parts, which may not fit with your concept of the finished bike at all.

Rob: The café racer has certain distinctive features; so what is your particular philosophy of this style?
Martyn: Some design features are mandatory; such as there must be a straight line from the lower edge of the fuel tank and the seat; and a solo seat at that. That is why the rear of the frame needs to be right. The front wheel/tyre needs to be roughly the same size as the rear, and the back of the seat needs to line up with the back axle, give or take an inch. Clip-ons or low handlebars give the look, which is taken from the racing bikes of the 1960s. Once those criteria are met, the line blurs and you can let your creativity loose.
Rob: So what made you use the GT750 as the centrepiece of your second build, and how much of the original bike did you use?
Martyn: The GT750 is one of the most well-known two strokes of all time, and extremely iconic of the last of the big two strokes from the 1970s. Also, I had the advantage of having Dave Cooper working alongside me, who has experience with bike tuning on a professional scale. As

for the engine itself, it's a beautiful piece of engineering inside and out, and here in the Midlands we have the advantage of having an expert who spends most of his time working on them and providing parts. This has enabled us to take the engine from a standard tune and more up to the tune of the race version of the TR engine.

I decided to use the engine and frame but everything else would be radically different. I removed the 750 swingarm and suspension and fitted the monoshock arrangement from a CBR400RR. I had mentally eyed up this piece of kit and knew that it was roughly the same width with a bit of jiggling, but I had to strengthen the frame at the point where the monoshock joined it. I welded in some steel stress gussets and made an aluminium block from billet for the shock to attach to. For the front suspension, I chose the glitzy and chunky-looking legs from the ZX10R, but polished off the gold finish on a lathe, as the colour wasn't going to fit in with my overall colour scheme. The rear wheel is from a Kawasaki ER6F but the drive sprocket is by Talon Engineering and is anodised gold. Talon started out making hubs for speedway and grass track some forty years ago.

Rob: Exactly what is that finish on the tank and seat, and do you start by doing drawings for your project?

Martyn: The finish of the fuel tank and seat were the main items for setting the colour scheme, and I had both of them nickel plated at Genius of the Lamp over in the Jewellery Quarter, Birmingham. Nickel finish is not so harsh a lustre as plain aluminium, having a sort of pale straw gold sheen to its finish. Genius of the Lamp is known for being a high quality restorer and finisher of specialised lamps for vintage cars. The fuel tank is from a Royal Enfield and the shape was just right for the look I wanted; and no I don't do drawings, I just have a concept that is in my head and I work from that but it's a flexible concept like most creations. Sometimes you simply stumble across a part such as a tank or fitting and know that it is just right for that bike.

Rob: Brackets, lugs, whatever you call them, are the unsung heroes of the bike set-up aren't they? But when you strip a bike ready to fit unfamiliar parts such as fuel tank and seat, then you have to decide how these parts are going to be held on?

Martyn: Quite. The new brackets have to be well thought through when you do a dry run of popping all the ancillary parts such as seat and fuel tank in place. The brackets have to look professional, i.e. good welded joints, have an aesthetic look too, and especially if they are on show. However, in truth, these seemingly mundane brackets have an important role to play in the look and the final safe use of the bike. And safety is just one of those programmes you have to have running in your head at every stage of the build. Then at times you design a bracket and end up not liking it after staring at it for a while. That happened to the hanger brackets for the exhausts. The aluminium seat support for instance has to be strongly attached to the rear of the frame, so there I drilled through the sheet metal into the frame, then tapped a thread in the frame so that all the bolts then screw straight into it.

Rob: You say that the engine has been tuned to race standard. What exactly does that entail?

Martyn: On the timing picture you may just be able to see that an extra 2.5mm spacer has been fitted between the barrels and the crankcase. Add two gaskets to this thickness and you raise the ports up and alter the porting timing. This was where Dave had to calculate the volume in the crankcases, the squish volume (that's the volume

A Suzuki GT750 – but not as we know it.

Opposite top left:
Battery and electrics neatly hidden under seat.

Opposite top right:
Carburettors.

Opposite below: **Clutch, thumb brake and control.**

between piston at TDC and head when fastened down – and don't forget that the spark plug interior is 1cc, and open up the ports a fraction. Port positions and timing, that is to say where the port (transfer and exhaust) positions are in relation to the piston movement, is critical on a two stroke. Only then can the ignition timing be fixed. Add to this the fact that I had the crank balanced and lightened (Chris Applebee Engineering of Basildon) and the pistons and con rods, too.

Rob: You mentioned safety as an important consideration? Where else did that come into play?

Martyn: Every detail, every nut and bolt has to be thought through, to make the bike safe, that's besides the big stuff of steering geometry and engine building.

Our build principle is always to over-engineer. So, for instance, in the choice of nuts and bolts used. Also, the bracket that takes the load from the monoshock is made from the strongest material we could get, and the headstock was seam welded, whereas before it was just tacked. All this adds to a safe bike to ride, and don't forget, this is going to be a fast machine.

Rob: Any changes to the gearbox?

Martyn: Only that I had the third and fourth gears made of a stronger steel, again C.A. Engineering. The original bike did occasionally have a problem where the dogs wore down, and I didn't want that to happen.

Rob: The engine looks highly polished. What was the final finish?

Martyn: After the crankcases were vapour blasted, I decided to create a finish that would resist any oil stains, so I used an aluminium primer and finish made by VHT. Other engine cases have been highly polished.

Rob: So Martyn, I have sat on the bike and it looks and feels a truly great machine, except I find the handgrips a little bit harsh to the touch. Now I don't expect you to let me have a test drive since there are only 8 miles on the clock and the build was nearly ten grand; so you will have to tell me, what's the ride like?

Martyn: Occasionally with a bike that is all about looks, form takes over a little from function, and the milled handgrips are hard but the answer to that is to wear gloves. Any serious motorcyclist should always wear gloves anyway. I have to say honestly that the ride is good; we got the geometry spot on. The engine is gorgeous, powerful and smooth, and we just need to tweak a few things on the carburettors to get a smooth response right through the rev range. Also I am so pleased the electrics work superbly, so right now I'm looking forward to getting it a MOT and out on the road. And as someone I know is fond of saying, 'See you out there'.

2WHEELSMIKLOS

SPAIN/UK

2WheelsMiklos is a close-knit band of three guys based in Guildford, Surrey. Miklos (Mike) Salamon is the founder and owner, and focuses on sourcing bikes, parts and sales. Alan Wells and Dave are talented men with lifetimes of technical motorcycling experience, and they run the workshop. The 2WheelsMiklos collection has been driven by two concepts. Firstly, to find, ride and restore the iconic bikes of the twentieth century centred around my era, which is exciting for all of us aging baby boomers. Secondly, to include an example of as many types of motorcycle engine as possible.

Miklos tell his story:

'Most of my school friends were bikers, and bikes were what we relied on for day-to-day transport. My first bike, bought in 1973 in Johannesburg, was a 1961 AJS 500 single. This was my ride until 1979. I loved the thumper and its various oddities. Of course, I lusted after many of the great bikes of the late 1960s, '70s and early '80s. However, financial circumstances and my gallivanting to and from work at various distant mines meant that all I could do was dream of these machines. In 1981 I bought a brand new and very functional Honda CX500 and my wife and I toured extensively on it, including doing the infamous Buffalo Rally to Port Elizabeth, South Africa, in 1983.

'Then came a break from biking, as family and career took precedence (I think many of us are familiar with this tale, too). However, I always wanted back, so in 1995 I bought a Kawasaki VN-15, the biggest capacity production bike at the time. I was again hooked, and so the following year bought a "grey" market 1996 Heritage Softail Harley. So started my love affair with Harleys, also shared by my wife. We were founder members of the Johannesburg Hog Chapter in 1997 and then also joined the Surrey, UK (now Hogsback) Chapter in 1999. Progressively over the next dozen years new bikes were added, both in Johannesburg and in Surrey, typically cruisers with big engines. A bike that had made a huge impression on me in my school days was the Triumph Bonneville, elegant and sexy but at the same time (in my view) a bit of an aggressive hooligan. In 1998 I managed to buy a 1970 T120R in Johannesburg. This came with us to Surrey in 1999 as it was much more realistic to do the restoration in the UK. Over the next ten or so years Arthur at Rockerbox (in Farnham, Surrey) brought it back to its former glory. This was the bike that got me thinking it could be possible to live out the dreams of all the bikes that I had missed out on in my youth.

2WheelsMiklos's personal take on the Bonneville.

A Bonneville in the true scramble style.

'In 2012 my formal business life wound down and now, given time, I decided to have a real go at the classic bike scene. My objectives were to find, restore and ride the great bikes of my era. My view on restoration was that the machines should be mechanically and electrically sound and good bikes to ride. They should also be pretty shiny and good-looking. I am not wedded to originality for the sake of originality. I also have a real interest in different engine configurations, so some bikes have been added to the collection mainly because they are different. Given that I am a mining engineer and not a mechanical engineer, I reckoned that the restorations would be mine to manage, but not actually do. So the process started, and the number of bikes and associated projects grew apace. Along the way it became apparent that the collection would rapidly outgrow the room available at my home (yep, got that), and I also realised that I really wanted to get more personally involved in the actual restoration work.

'This led to taking premises at Astra House in Cranleigh, the establishment of a pretty serious workshop and recruiting Alan Wells to lead the work and to teach me. The collection now has a philosophy and structure underpinning it, and at the time of writing this potted history numbers twenty-nine bikes, 90 per cent of which have been completed. This has proven to be pretty successful and has attracted a lot of support and help from my family. Hence the foundation was laid for the next phase, where the full collection and workshop is housed together and we start to do restorations and customisations for others. This will be realised with the opening of 2WheelsMiklos at Stag Hill.'

'Alan Wells, born and bred in Sussex, has been the technical brains behind the 2WheelsMiklos collection since mid-2013. His bigger projects have been the Honda Four, Yamaha XS1100E, black bomber, Sunbeam and the Kawasaki H1A. He has also made very significant improvements to the Moto Guzzi 850T, Benelli 750 Sei and Suzuki GT750. His current focus is on our customs: the two BMWs (R80/7 & K100RT) and the Harley 1200 Sportster. Alan got into bikes through the influence of his father. When he was a mere 12 years old, they acquired a Thunderbird, which they totally restored. This was the catalyst for further joint projects and ultimately projects of his own, both restorations and modifications. After leaving school Alan went into the motor trade as a Land Rover technician, as at the time there was no motorbike technician training to be had.

'This led to working with various specialist vehicles, and then back into motorbikes. His focus was customs and choppers. Through the years a good many of his creations have been prizewinners and have also been photographed for and written up by various magazines. He then worked for a Triumph dealer for seven years, whilst in parallel developing his own business making specialist parts for the custom bike world. Alan's particular passion is motorcycle racing and he has through the years technically supported various disciplines. For the past two years this has encompassed a team entered in the Triumph Triple Challenge, which, as from 2014, has also been part sponsored by 2WheelsMiklos.

'Dave is from West Sussex and has been in the motor industry all his working life. After a four-year City and Guilds apprenticeship he qualified as a mechanic. Throughout this period he worked for various original equipment manufacturers. Then came a seven-year stint as an AA patrolman. This experience has made Dave very streetwise, he will get almost any vehicle going if he has to! After this he and his wife moved to Orlando in Florida, where Dave ultimately had his own garage and body shop. During the eighteen years he was there he also got himself into a number of more exciting pursuits; for example drag racing converted saloon cars, spannering for a schoolboy motocross team, racing quarter-mile dirt ovals and power boating. In 2010 Dave and family (wife and two daughters) returned to the UK, and he worked principally in

a body shop until joining 2WheelsMiklos in June 2014. Given the complementary nature of Dave's and Alan's experience base, their respective focus, in very broad terms, is Alan on the customs and Dave on the restorations.

'2WheelsMiklos is a business developed from a passion for the motorcycling icons of the 1940s to the 1980s. It started in 2012 as a private project to recreate the icons of Miklos' era. From there, our team recognised that some of these bikes could become so much more than the original. Hence, the addition of the custom bikes. After two years working out of scattered premises we now run our operations out of Stag Hill as a fully integrated motorcycle restoration and customisation shop on one site. Also on the site is the 2WheelsMiklos collection of icons – displayed to whet the appetite and also to take a journey down memory lane. In addition to the classics and customs we are also the regional sales and service agent for Metisse Motorcycles, focused on the Metisse Desert Racer, the Bonneville-engined, Rickman-framed scrambler made famous by Steve McQueen.'

Certain bikes captured the imagination through their innovation and engineering prowess or simply by just being superbly fit for purpose. These represent the historic foundation on which the 2WheelsMiklos collection has been built. So, I have kept their best, in my mind, bikes for last; just savour the fabulous pictures on the next few pages for they feature a resurrected Rocket 3, the classic 2.3L Triumph, the biggest bruiser on the road. It crashed in April 2015 and was back on the road, much altered you understand, only two months

Valkyrie and Rocket.

later. I'm sure you will agree that's an achievement. And then we have their equally amazing Valkyrie, where the engine alone is a work of engineering beauty. Finally we have a gorgeous Honda CB900F café racer in chrome (and there was me thinking that chrome had had its day, we all make mistakes eh?). I have, with 2Wheels' great assistance, also been able to show here some of the build process. Wow.

Left top: **Crash damage – oh dear.**

Left bottom: **Receiving some TLC.**

Right and above: **The Rocket 3: Bobbed front and rear mudguard; custom belly pan. Roadster foot controls and handle bar Motogadget indicators. Pearl black and white paintwork by Cycle Sprays.**

Left top: **Working on exhausts.**

Left below: **Much improved.**

Above and right: **The Valkyrie six into one exhaust system with a SuperTrapp at the end. Rocket 3 tail light and bespoke seat. Handlebar with risers, integrated GPS, relocked stock instruments, bespoke idiot lights and bar end indicators.**

Clockwise from left:

Honda CB900F rear suspension detail.

Part of the build process.

What a fabulous engine.

Honda CB900F in café racer trim.

Right: **Here the design brief was build a muscular but elegant bike – rideable too. Triumph Trophy forks and wheels; Harris clip-ons. Styling – a chrome tank; Kawasaki Z1 tailpiece – what else? Norvil nose cone; Marving 4 into 2 headerpipes plus in-house silencers. Paintwork: Metal flake containing pearl white – very special, and beautiful in sunlight.**

UNDERKOVER

6/5/4 MOTORS

6/5/4 Motors is a bike-building company based in Stockholm run by Johan Orrestedt, Johan Nordin and Daniel Jakobsson, who turn mainly old bikes into high-quality café racers, scramblers and street trackers. Together they started to build bikes in 2012 and became a business two years later. They have a 600m² garage in Södermalm, Stockholm that is situated below Johan Orrestedt's surf shop. This garage is divided into two parts, one where 6/5/4 Motors wrenches bikes for clients, and one where it rents out space for people who want to work on their own custom bikes. The latter currently has forty tenants.

'We build customised motorcycles, mainly motorcycles with knobby tyres (scramblers) since we think the best way to enjoy a motorcycle ride is in the dirt.'

The Ducati

This cool green Ducati 860 GT is one of their best from the workbench, and it's as cool as a combination of chocolate and mint; in fact you may wish to ride it and then eat it. The guys had some very particular ideas for the project, so they settled on the GT as a donor.

'The spectacular engine with its unmistakeable V twin design, the iconic tank and that flat frame line were too good to overlook,' they say.

However, finding an 860 GT in Sweden seemed like an impossible task but after a month of hunting around, the team struck gold with a mid-1970s GTS variant. The owner was a Ducati aficionado who had kept the bike in a barn for years, so it took huge promises to keep the bike 'more or less' original to pry it from his hands.

The BMW

Despite the odd location, 6/5/4 Motors serves up some fine Scandinavian design in two-wheeled form, this time with a clean and minimal BMW R75/5.

Johan gives us the process:

'The Beemer arrived in the workshop a couple of years ago but it had been standing unused for two decades. So task numero uno was to get it running. Then, a prospective customer, a psychologist, came along, specifically looking for an R75. You see bikes are as good for the mind as they are for the soul.'

Opposite: **The BMW '75.**

'He had a few minor requests but was happy to leave everything else to us guys. Designs were drawn up and the deal was sealed. To get the bike into shape, the R75 was torn down to the nuts and bolts, the engine was overhauled, the valves adjusted, a new electronic ignition installed, and the timing set. To keep it running sweet, a new battery was installed in a custom-made box under the swingarm. The exhaust was upgraded with a set of reverse-cone mufflers. Next, the guys fabricated a new subframe, narrower and shorter than stock. The rest of the frame was de-tabbed and cleaned up, then sandblasted and repainted. The seat is a one-off, covered in velvety nubuck leather. As you'd expect from the Swedes, the cockpit is supremely de-cluttered. The bulky BMW switches have been chucked in favour of mini-switches, with the wiring running inside the MX-style bars – neat. The ignition is Motogadget's ultra-convenient keyless m-Lock system. A Daytona Velona speedo and Biltwell Inc. grips keep things minimal and stylish. The lighting has been slimmed down, too; Bates-style head and tail lights now cut through the dark Stockholm nights, flanked by mini turn signals.'

The Ducati café racer.

For the mudguards – yes, look closely – a pair of Triumph Bonneville items have been severely bobbed. The shocks are from Hagon, and the tyres are Bridgestone Trailwings with a trials-type pattern.

It's a tasteful set of modifications, but it's the paint scheme that really sets this BMW apart. 6/5/4 mixed the mint-and-turquoise combo for the frame themselves – and it's the only splash of colour. The rest of the R75 is black, with just off-white for the lights, and a mix of raw and polished finishes for the engine. The tank is matt black with a white pinstripe, and there's a 6/5/4 logo in place of the usual BMW roundel. There's a crisp elegance to this build, which seems to be a developing 6/5/4

signature. However, despite the extreme cleanliness, it's a bike that gets ridden regularly.

Outdoor images by David Gonzalez.

Into the Woods: A Triumph Bonneville Scrambler

So Johan, tell us how this Bonneville came to be:

'Under the engine covers, there's not much difference between the Triumph Bonneville and

Scrambler. Other than their firing intervals (the Scrambler has a 270-degree crank for extra 'thump'), the bikes are mainly separated by styling cues. Which means that, with a few well-placed mods, a stock Bonnie can be made as dirt-worthy as a Scrambler. A client was bored with his stock 2007 Bonneville and wanted something more suitable to off-road excursions, so he took it in for an overhaul.

'He works as a sailor on a tugboat in the North Sea. He spends four weeks at sea, and four weeks on land, riding his new Bonnie Scrambler in the woods outside of Stockholm.'

6/5/4's Swedish pride led them to the Öhlins catalogue for a suspension boost at both ends, complete with new triple clamps to hold the beefy, upside-down forks. Pirelli Scorpion rally tyres were chosen to p fling mud. The guys then tweaked the Triumph's lines by raising the rear of the fuel tank slightly to straighten it out. They also built a new seat on a plastic moulded base, covering it in black leather. Out back, the frame rails were trimmed down slightly and mounts added for the turn signals. The rear fender and the slimmer side covers are JVB Moto parts. The most obvious visual cue is the Arrow two-into-one exhaust system, an aftermarket part specific to the Scrambler.

Fitting it meant relocating the Bonneville's rear brake fluid reservoir and fabricating a hanger on which to mount the silencer. The bike is kitted with a whole host of delectable parts: Biltwell Inc. Mushman foot pegs, Grimeca controls, MX-style 'fatbars' mounted on new clamps, a new headlight and a tiny MMB speedo. The front brake has been upgraded with a braided steel hose, and a new disc. A full complement of Motogadget components has been installed too, including m-Switches, an m-Lock keyless ignition and m-Relay+ flasher relays.

6/5/4 had a few pieces in mind that couldn't be sourced, so it turned to CAD and waterjet cutting to produce them. These included the skid plate, licence plate bracket and fork protectors, as well as a set of super-short headlight brackets. (A set of headlight brackets had already been bought, but they 'made the bike look a bit piggy-like with a big snout'.)

DIAMOND ATELIER

GERMANY

Tom Konecny (23) – Founder, creative director, designer, mechanic. Pablo Steigleder (25) – Founder, head fabricator, mechanic.

So this is how it all starts – Tom Konecny and Pablo Steigleder are cruising along one summer's evening through the urban sprawl of downtown Munich, looking for and finding the local bikers' hangout. They cut their engines and look around, only to be disappointed with the regular display of half-standard machines having all the same kind of bolt on accessories that come straight out of a catalogue. What gets to them is that the bikes they see all look as though they have all recently rolled off the same café racer production line.

Tom and Pablo knew that they could do better, but how? Yes, they both have a passion for motorcycling, and have worked on bikes together since they were sixteen. Yes, they have fresh ideas coupled with youthful enthusiasm and a vision of what could be done, but spannering activities, and the old hands on approach to engineering knowledge were not going to cut it in the twenty-first century. So, they took the brave step of getting themselves into Munich's University to study economics and engineering; academic activities that would give them

the technical ability they required to make their dream a reality.

Tom continues their story:

'Now suitably equipped, we founded Diamond Atelier with a 0.17-carat diamond being set into the upper fork clamp; this would be our signature style for all future builds. This was the summer of 2013 and we dived straight into the deep end with our first custom bike DA#1 taken from a base BMW R80 RT. Quickly there were invitations to various motorcycling events including Motorrad Days, Glemseck 101, Puer and Crafted Festival; International Motorcycle Exhibition (IMOT), and, of course, establishing an important online presence via BikeExif, Highsnobiety, HYPEbeast, Blacklist, etc.'

Tom and Pablo then started to create one off, hand-built custom motorcycles with the main focus on what works, what looks good, and the proportions, plus a radical stance inspired by and drawn from the urban environment that surrounded them. Their first DA exhibition and after-show party was in Munich in January 2015, followed by the opening of their showroom in the city later that year.

Diamond Atelier riding scene.

The workshop with DA#1 front left.

Tom tells us how the Atelier #1 came to life:

'The Diamond Atelier #1 bike had naturally to stand out from the crowd to be different from all the other boxer airheads in the room. In order to do that, our two guys examined carefully the motorised world around at that time that included street fighters, professional racing models, track bikes and even drift spec cars. The result was a unique design of well-proportioned body components coupled with two base colours. This gave the BM an understated look but one that quickly got admiring looks. We mean to go on building great-looking bikes that are a joy to ride and be seen on.'

DA#3 BMW R100R

The third machine to come out of Tom and Pablo's workshop was the DA#3 – no surprise there. This bike

was built with the same styling principles and attention to detail. It takes the R100R to new heights, being much more than a collection of bolt-on goodies welded on to a distinct and iconic frame. The DA#3 is a dark delight that melts into the spirit of the night. Tom and Pablo were going to even greater success and distinction with this metal masterpiece. They took an original 1994 BMW, dumped the ghastly fuel tank and seat, and stood back to assess their blank canvas before remodelling with an R series. The riding position was on the way to being completely transformed. After designing a custom subframe and handcrafted single seat the build took on a darker and more menacing stance.

The unmistakeable look of the BMW boxer engine was also given a makeover with a pair of 40mm Dellorto carburettors and K&N filters. A stubby Akrapovic exhaust completed the rear end. Meanwhile the space between the fuel tank and engine, seat and rear wheel was cleared of all clutter to give the essential minimalistic lines of a true café racer.

The DA#1 from the side and above.

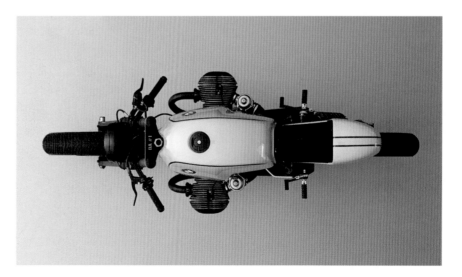

DA#3 Spec List
Restyled Triple Clamp
Tyres: Continental TKC80
LSL Style headlight
320mm Brembo floating disc brakes
Braided hoses
Clip-ons and rear sets
Stylish dash with DA's signature diamond and serial number, just in case you forget what you're riding – as if that was possible!

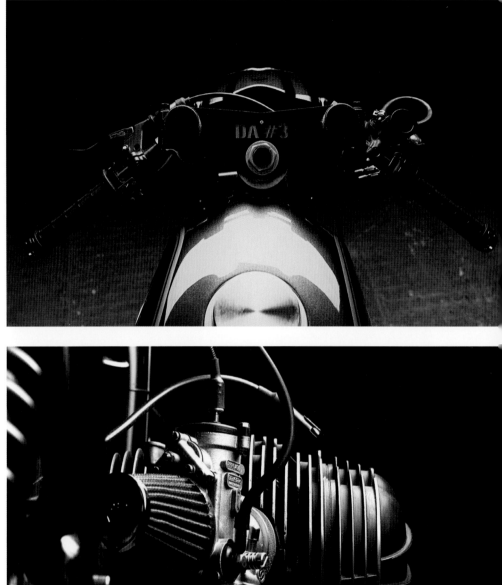

A mean and aggressive BMW – the DA#3.

DA#5 – Suzuki DR650, 1992

Following Diamond Atelier's launch into the custom motorcycle world, the pair received worldwide recognition for their work, especially on their unique BMW builds.

The BMW boxer airheads set the urban signature style of the young Munich brand. Part of this scene was the current trend of transforming road bikes into 'scramblers'. Tom and Pablo quickly grew tired of seeing the same models over and over again and decided to do a complete opposite – to transform a typical 1990's dirt bike into a full-blown Diamond Atelier café racer.

Tom relates the build:

> 'The focus of this build was to show the creativity, dedication and craftsmanship that is poured into every Diamond Atelier project.'

Therefore a Suzuki DR650 was the perfect donor – it was the bike furthest away from what the two founders considered good looking but with its high-capacity single hammer engine it had great potential.

Diamond Atelier had no fears about redesigning the complete chassis of the DR650 in order to receive the desired stance. This includes a heavily modified mainframe and completely hand-built rear frame, as well as a full custom suspension set-up and a rare set of racing wheels. To add to the agile and perfectly sleek silhouette the bike needs to cut through downtown city traffic, a front mask and seat cowling were hand-built to match the vintage 1970's gas tank. Low slung

The DA#5.

clip-ons and CNC machined rear sets came from ABM
and provide an aggressive seating position for the driver.

The DA#5 remains Diamond Atelier's most advanced
custom bike project to this day and is meant to show that
the bar on such transformations can still be raised.

DA#5 Specs list
Make/Model: Suzuki DR650 SP44B
Capacity: 650ccm
Engine power: 50hp

Chassis
Heavily modified mainframe with scratch-built rear
frame
Newly built up 41mm telescopic fork with new
internals and CNC-machined upper triple clamps
Re-spoked 17in racing rims on DR650 hubs
Metzeler Racetec RR racing slicks
Custom-made Wilbers rear shock
ABM Multiclip clip-ons
ABM Syntho levers
ABM grips
Customised ABM rear sets

Bodywork
Vintage 1970s gas tank
Hand-built front mask (1mm sheet metal)
Hand-built seat cowling (1mm sheet metal)
Genuine cowhide seat

Performance
Newly built-up and resealed engine
Re-jetted carbs

K&N air filter
Scratch-built header
SuperTrapp sport exhaust muffler
Castrol oils
320mm wave front brake disc
200mm wave rear brake disc
ABM stainless steel brake hoses
Customised Yamaha YZR-1 clutch control
Customised Suzuki GSX-R brake pump
Entire paint job done by hand in-house

Electronics
Completely new wiring with no battery
    (kick-start only)
Kellermann R3 flasher unit
Motogadget bar end indicators
Motogadget rear indicators
Motogadget speedometer

MAX HAZAN

USA

I have just watched one of Max's fabulous bikes on YouTube, a glorious, sleek 500cc Royal Enfield. He gently and lovingly lowers it down from the workbench on a pulley system. Then, he takes it out for a spin, after first pointing out some of its unique and amazing features. I love his stuff but I had to do a bit of homework to discover his particular path into the wondrous world of motorcycles. Max was fortunate as a child, a bit like Winston Yeh in having a DIY dad, that his dad bought him a Lego set. Not content to just let the parts fit together as they were designed, Max had to go one step further and melt them in the oven so that he could create shapes of his own. Then, like many young lads (me included), he built model airplanes, until it was time to leave school behind and get what certain grown-ups call a proper job – whatever that is. His first machine was a small dirt bike, ridden at the tender age of 3, and he later progressed on to the road with a Buell Lightning.

Opposite: **Max with his Ducati.**

Left: **Design and inspiration with a BSA.**

A Royal Enfield has never looked so wondrous.

As soon as Max had some money in his pocket, he started to build motorcycles as a hobby, until his father intervened – in the best possible way – and asked: 'So why don't you build bikes for a living?' So Max took that large leap of faith, a huge gamble with his future (along with a pay cut) and he hasn't looked back. He started out small with a windowless shop in Brooklyn, New York, splitting his work between carpentry on one side of the room and bits of bikes on the other. Gradually the bikes took over and grew in size, so he had to move into larger premises.

So, where did the inspiration come from?

'It came when I started experimenting with all sorts of mechanisms, and not being afraid of making some kind of crazy cross breed. For instance, I had a Honda Generator motor with automatic transmission from a golf cart that I made run on bicycle wheels. That thing did 90mph. Then I met a girl and moved to California. She asked me to go and she was worth it.

'Two of my best bikes were the Enfield and the Ironhead, where I started building from the engine outwards as it stood on the bench. I love looking at pictures of engines, and then get inspired by their shapes. I put the engine on the bench and start to imagine how the bike could look. You make mistakes along the way, sure, like everyone else, and you throw some of your designs in the bin; but you get there in the end.

'Later I bought a 1949 BSA single, in excellent condition, and I just knew that I could make a great bike out of it. And every now and then I get my woodworking tools out and use those skills to make things like the curved seat on the Royal Enfield. The inspiration for that came from those gorgeous Italian speedboats. My favourite bike, however, is the Brough Superior, and it's probably got something to do with that fabulous engine.

'As for the future, well I have settled down with Sarah, made some cool bikes, and won a few prestigious awards, so essentially I want to carry on doing what I do best: making unique two-wheeled machines.'

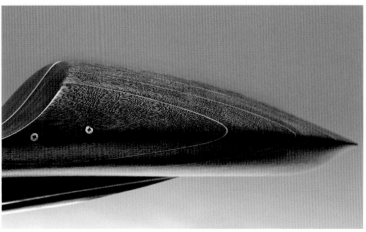

IT ROCKS!BIKES

PORTUGAL

Osvaldo Coutinho and Alexandre Santos, both engineers, based in Oporto, Portugal, are addicted to motorcycles, and have built bikes under the 'it roCkS!bikes' brand since the beginning of 2013. They wisely surround themselves with an exceptional technical team in specialised areas, but all design work is prepared directly by them, in detail.

Osvaldo explains their goals for bike building:

'We strive to keep our concepts simple, with clean and elegant lines, with a focus on good handling, something that not all custom bikes manufactures seem to focus much on. We work hard to create exclusive bikes, matching the classic style of café racers of the 1970s, with the dynamic and handling of actual sports bikes. The combination of the tank, seat and tail running in one piece, built in metal, combined with the accuracy of finishing and precision in assembly are our trademarks. All our bikes are unique and absolutely unrepeatable designs; we never produce two identical bikes. The only similarity is perhaps the style that preferentially promotes the café racer culture.'

XJR1300 Dissident

The company celebrated its twentieth anniversary of the street racer/bruiser with an awe-inspiring café racer creation, the yard-built XJR1300 Dissident.

The bike features it roCkS!bikes' signature monocoque design; that means a one-piece tank, seat and tail unit to you and me, with a handcrafted metal unit flowing from just behind the triple clamps all the way back to the end of the tail. YZF-R1 upside down forks are modified to fit the XJR1300 steering column. A host of Motogadget extras include clip-on café racer bars, aluminium grips, M-Blaze turn signals and a Motoscope pro dashboard on top of a custom CNC-machined aluminium bracket. Tasty stuff.

The bike rides on custom made spoke wheels, has an ISR braking system, including master cylinders for front brake and clutch, front and rear callipers, and massive 340mm front discs; 267mm rear discs and 6-piston calipers with Hell Performance steel mesh brake and clutch hoses. Stylish engine covers with glass windows allow you to see into the heart of the machine, a feature rarely seen; but watching machinery working is always a fascinating sight. A small high-performance oil cooler

keeps everything at the correct temperature and a handmade 4-2 stainless steel exhaust makes all the noise one requires. An Aluminium 'Monza' gas cap along with an integrated tuning fork symbol 'medallion' set on the tank provides a bit of two-wheel bling, while the finishing touch is an artisan-made leather seat.

Yard-Built VMAX Gasoline

The monocoque masters kicked off 2016 in style with their third yard-built project, based on the legendary Yamaha VMAX.

For their latest creation, Osvaldo and Alex set out to give the VMAX an entirely new image, enhancing and exploiting its drag racing capabilities. As with all their builds, the CS_07 Gasoline gets the trademark monocoque unit, although as the VMAX fuel tank is located under the seat, the unit features a false fuel tank. The unit is handcrafted from metal sheet and gives the bike a sleeker, slimmer and sportier profile with a retro style.

The drag racer influence is clear to see with the massive slick rear Mickey Thomson tyre and handmade stainless steel 4-2 headers connecting to a custom free flow SC Project exhaust system with carbon silencers.

The CS_07 Gasoline rides on custom-made spoke wheels, 3.5 × 18in front with 120/70 × 18in Dunlop rubber and a 6.0 × 18in rear for the drag strip tyre. The stock tacho is kept but comes in a custom aluminium housing, and the standard fuel tank is replaced with a beautiful custom aluminium unit with it roCkS!bikes motif. A metal handcrafted fairing ensures slippery aerodynamics for the ¼ mile and LSL footpeg adapters and clip-ons put the rider in the correct position. A Rizoma fuel cap and K&N air filter add some extra bling and Brembo brake and clutch master cylinders take it to the next level.

A host of Motogadget parts including handlebar grips, an m-Switch and m-Blaze turn signals ensure

the custom work really stands out, and the handmade leather seat with it roCkS!bikes logo sets the standard.

The build was completed at the end of 2015, the last of the year to celebrate thirty years of the VMAX. To mark the milestone a classic paint job was used to finish the bike. Taken from the 1970s, the white, black and yellow colour scheme is pure icon, celebrating not just thirty years of the VMAX, but also sixty years of Yamaha! The bike was airbrushed and then gloss varnished in-house by the builders.

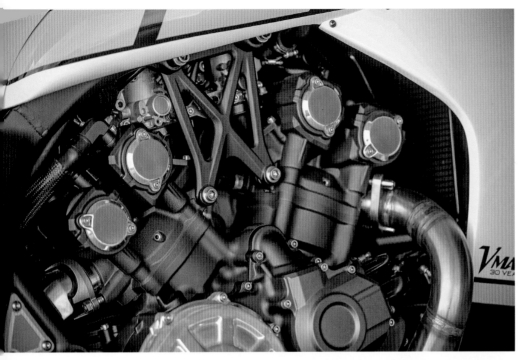

LORNE CHEETHAM'S KICKBACK CUSTOM BIKE SHOW

UK

Here in Britain we are blessed with a wealth of motorcycle shows and auto jumbles where you can view a plethora of what motorcycling has to offer, including the most expensive, the rarest, and the most wonderful. But (and it is a big but) where does the custom bike get a look in? Lorne Cheetham's Kickback Custom Bike Show seems to have gone from strength to strength since its launch in 2010, judging solely from the number of visiting motorcycles and cars in the capacious car park at Cheltenham Racecourse.

Under tolerable skies, and an almost decent trip down the M5 from Brum to Cheltenham, Jane and I (that's my wife by the way) strolled with anticipation into a dazzling showroom of simply wonderful bikes. This show, designed to show off the UK's best fabricators, designers and custom engineers, certainly kept us fascinated for hours. The main auditorium was decorated with examples of what our finest small companies can produce in the way of custom bikes, from Bantams right up to custom Z1000s. Prizes were handed out to a whole range of styles from café racers to steampunk, and I have included a couple of fine chops to demonstrate that the chopper as a style is certainly not dead; it's lying low but is still a desirable class of two-wheeled machinery.

I was particularly impressed by Chris Roberts's home-built (he works for a gas company) steampunk V Twin. I have to admit that 'steampunk' was a new one to me, but I love it. It's a delicious combination of Victorian technology, horology, Heath Robinson, and sheer creative genius. And you can spend several happy and instructive hours discovering all the oddities of Chris's creation.

Opposite: **The artwork on the fuel tank alone is exquisite ...**

Above: **Entrance to the showroom.**

Clockwise from left:

Vintage Vincent and customised Yamaha – an unlikely duo.

Chopped Triumph from Oily Rag.

Trophy winners – a beautifully chopped Harley by Rolling Art Motorcycles' Glenn and Gary Dance.

Suzuki Bandit by Trevor Weeks – built over two years. Artwork by Joeby, and now owned by Jo Brakes – lucky Jo.

Back to Chris Roberts' 'Steampunk' – drool over those faux wooden wheels, and underneath a leather seat well worth admiring.

Martyn Wilkins, Steve and me with Martyn's wonderful Suzuki GT750.

OLD EMPIRE MOTORCYCLES

UK

OEM's custom motorcycle concept builds are complete one-offs, and the guys, Alec Sharp and Rafe Pugh, admit that countless hours are devoted to each project regardless of the style and donor motorcycle. They have found that it is important that each and every bike that leaves the OEM House of Assembly is a true Old Empire Motorcycle, and this is why they take so much time, considering each build and whether it is suitable to be part of this very special breed of OEM motorcycles.

Alec explains what OEM is about:

'Old Empire Motorcycles came about through an absolute and enduring passion for everything two-wheeled, and The House of Assembly (HOA) is where we pay daily homage to the gods of speed and fuel. It's the place we meet, greet, drill, weld, cut, grind, turn, mill, hammer, roll and notch to our hearts content to create and display our bespoke motorcycles. Unlike most custom bike builders in the UK we do not stick to styling "rules" but focus on creating the very best we possibly can with what we are given. We create a handful of one-off custom bikes annually that all take their names from Great British automotive, aeronautic and maritime history, a slight nod of recognition to the people who designed and built these machines

for us to be inspired by today. We also appreciate that individuals have their own conceptual ideas that they may want to see taken from paper and turned into steel, therefore it only seemed sensible to also offer our skills and services in a way in which people could do just that. It's a bit like a recipe really; take me and Rafe Pugh, for instance; add a dose of general education, a liberal sprinkling of motorcycle savvy, eight ounces of raw talent and another eight ounces of artistic ability, add two pounds of sheer dedication, stir briskly and allow to gel in a suitably kitted out garage, and voila, the result is a steady supply of amazing bikes.'

Alec is the one who generally deals with the design and creation of Old Empire Motorcycles (OEM) builds.

He continues:

'It's the perfect opportunity; to make exactly what we feel is required without cutting any corners. The creation of our other builds and our branding comes from both of us, plus a few other very dedicated British designers, craftspeople who we have the pleasure of working alongside. Rafe's talents lie in being able to create a story around the build, and then realise the imagery and clothing to

Taking the Typhoon out for a spin. The finish on this deep burgundy paintwork is to die for.

match, not forgetting being the main man behind the leatherwork and saddles. It's been a bloody good combination so far.'

The Typhoon

Alec and Rafe usually draw upon inspiration from specific styles, but with the Typhoon they have been inspired by the specific donor, in this case a Ducati 900ss.

Rafe tells the story:

'It is what we feel is the perfect showcase of the very best aesthetics from the original motorcycle, mixed with carefully engineered handmade components, to produce a bike that goes back to the very fundamentals of two-wheeled travel. The bike boasts a high-performance 904cc air-cooled L-twin engine, and it looks like it belongs to a modern art museum.'

Personally, I have to say that I absolutely love the look of this machine. I have, of course, no idea what it's like to ride, and probably never will, but just look at that colour, that design! There is the merest hint of steampunk in the handmade custom brass headlight, along with that awesome girder fork front end. Other superb details include a custom speedo and tacho set-up, the 21in front wheel quad leading shoe drum brake, custom bars, a bevel gear throttle, twin Amal GP3 carbs and a custom stainless exhaust system. And don't forget that amazing handmade seat, fuel tank, as well as the extended (and tasteful) use of brass and leather all across the bike.

It's almost Chicara, but more affordable, and probably more useable, too.

In the words of OEM's Alec Sharp:

> 'It's one of those machines that you only really feel comfortable on at speed, tucked in, feet up on the go-faster pegs and laid down over the tank. On that subject, it's still insanely fast, loud and handles surprising well.'

The bike was built over a period of eighteen months or so. Alec just added or made bits as and when he felt the need to, trying not to force the design or mindlessly stick to a self-imposed deadline. He says:

> I have found that, for me, this is the best way of going about building and designing something that is a little special.'

SPEC: Custom girder forks, and a custom speedo and tacho set-up. Custom brass headlight, the 21in front wheel quad leading shoe drum brake and single leading shoe drum. Custom bars, a bevel gear throttle, twin Amal GP3 carbs and a custom stainless exhaust system. Handmade rear sets, leather grips, a custom twin tanks with kneepads, fuel lines, a braided wiring loom, a pull-type starter and a handmade headlight shroud.

If someone should ever leave me a shedload of money I'm off down south to see this pair of geniuses.

The Merlin

The Merlin is the Japanese take on a 650cc parallel twin, and provides the perfect basis upon which this gentleman's 'café brat' is built around. The Merlin sits on plenty of Coker rubber in a stance that has been manipulated to get a suitably aggressive angle of attack, although its colour scheme using deep dark greens and gold's gives the overall build a refined and subtle look and feel.

Rafe tells the story:

'The Merlin was our first attempt at a custom parallel twin and our first Kawasaki W650 that we worked on. We were approached by the customer, who is based in Amsterdam, after them seeing a few of our previous builds and liking our styling and attention to detail. After a bit of toing-and-froing with emails and some skyping we had a good idea on where we wanted to go within the build. It's nice when dealing with people who genuinely love our styling and trust us implicitly when designing and deciding where to go within a build. Although much was sent over using our build idea sheet, it was left to us to ultimately come up with a design to take the W650 somewhere we felt it had had not been before, even though it's a donor used prolifically in Japan, on the Continent and in Australia.

'Looking at the stock frame and engine layout it became clear why it's favoured for a custom build, it lends itself to a variety of modifications, many

The Merlin

of which you can see on the Internet. From café racer to flat tracker to bobber, there is potential of creating a great custom motorcycle going down any of these avenues. However, we were not after creating just another great motorcycle, what we wanted to conceive needed to be the best custom W650 in terms of design and functionality. It's always best to aim high, as we have found through previous experience. The first thing to sort was the stance, which was achieved by dropping the front using a set of Ducati USD forks, and although the stock rims are both 18in rims we installed a wider front rim to accommodate the same size Coker tyres front and back. The blunt end was raised an inch or so using a set of custom Hagon shocks to give a slightly streetfighter element and achieve that acute angle of attack.

'Fabrication wise, although it may look much unmodified there was significant workshop time and design time getting that minimal rear cowling just right so the lines flow perfectly and the little LED rear light sunk in just right. The original tank retains its front mounts but we raised the rear end a good way to get that top line running nicely from the yoke down the tank into the seat and off the rear cowling. Making a custom seat pan that acts as the electrics box cover and installing some handmade gussets front and back to keep everything flowing was critical in keeping the bike in proportion. The tank also features indents in which leather scallops have been inserted as well as the bottom of the tank featuring a welded in skirt that hides the ugly box section top tube.

'We managed to keep all the controls stock, with the addition of some hand-dyed leather wrap and some scotching. Front lighting comes in the form of a big Bates headlight and peak and the customer asked for mini LED indicators, which we mounted as discreetly as possible. We also decided to work with our friends at Smiths again to make up an OEM grey-faced kph speedo that, safe to say, looks mighty fine integrated into the custom top yoke. Unfortunately the aluminium was so badly tarnished we decided on a new course of action by which the engine was masked up and the crankcases repainted a high temperature satin silver with the barrels and head going satin black with polished fins. The casings were then fine scotched and the rebuilt carbs with custom air filters installed to leave the engine looking

Rafe Pugh.

fantastic. Exhausts were handmade from tubular bends and rigged together and wrapped to stop them melting your leg (we will be making a proper stainless guard soon as it still melts your leg a little bit). Mini baffles with a good deal of sound-deadening material installed take the edge off what is a fantastic-sounding engine.

'The finishing came in the form of powder coating satin black the frame, swingarm and a few other components. All the plating went for chroming then once back was quickly scotched to produce a satin or brushed chrome effect. The paintwork deserves special attention, as it has to be seen to be properly appreciated. Greg from Black Shuck Kustoms, under our instructions, lead loaded the tank where it needed it and then removed the powder coat from the relevant panel work on the frame to leave a bare metal-brushed finish. After that it is a bit of a mystery how he achieved the fantastic dark green smoky bare metal high gloss finish with gold pinstriping but, whatever, it suits the bike down to the ground and has to be seen to be believed. Thanks goes to Black Shuck Kustoms, MP Blasting, Audrey Upholstery, Mark Bunning and Demeanour customs.'

2001 Kawasaki W650

Heavily modified frame

Ducati USD front end

Ducati brake caliper/disc

Ducati triple trees/modified top yoke

Coker 18in tyres front and back

Custom OEM leather battery satchel

Original control units

Heavily modified tank with leather panels

Custom seat with triple diamond stitching

New lengthened shocks

Custom tail light

Warning LED lights

Smiths/OEM grey-faced speedo

Ducati clip-ons

Custom electrics box

Custom wiring loom

Scotched aluminium rims/hubs

Fully rebuilt wheels with stainless steel spokes

Painted, scotched and fully serviced engine

Custom filters

Custom twin exhaust with mini baffles

Bates headlight with peak

LED indicators front and back

Brooks custom-dyed grip wrap

RACCIA MOTORCYCLES

USA

Michael LaFountain has been building vintage motorcycles since he was 17 years old. In 2006, he formed Raccia to create unique motorcycles heavily influenced by the race bikes of the 1950s, '60s and early '70s. On this particular example, the seat, oil tank, rearsets, pipes, levers, etc. are all handcrafted. Michael has, he admits, an obsessive desire to create, and an understated passion for motorcycles – full stop. He says:

"The bringing together of Raccia's handmade parts, reshaped stock parts and an obscene amount of time creating new lines is what makes these motorcycles one of a kind.'

History and Build Sheet for the 1976 Honda CB750, aka 'The Cold War'

Michael tells the story:

'This build started when I was contacted by Ryan Reynolds, the well-known Canadian actor, who asked me to build him a very special Honda. He is an avid rider/collector but the bike that started it all was his 76 CB750. It was the first bike he owned and learned how to ride as a teenager. He asked if I could build him a 76 (also his birth year) so he could take a trip back in time and rekindle the magic he had felt as a young kid with all the freedom in the world and not enough money in his pocket do anything about it.

'Originally this bike was going to be quite different but one of my favourite aspects of creating motorcycles is that you start down one path then take a wrong turn and end up in some weird town, make a U-turn, cross the tracks, find the interstate and end in a better place then you originally intended. My original plan was to create something more tailored and reminiscent of my typical works. In the early stages I received a few photos from Ryan of things that inspired him. To my surprise they were of items that were somewhat rough with heavy patina. Then he suggested the possibility of doing a raw tank. At first I wasn't feeling any enthusiasm. It's not exactly my forte, and it's kind of a trend these days to take a stock tank with no dings or dents sand it down to the bare metal and call it a day. But after a few hours of staring at the bike, I realised I had the opportunity to create something I had wanted to create for years.

'Since the very beginning I have lived by a motorcycle code, if you will. A motorcycle should be as impressive and aesthetically pleasing to the eye in its raw form before all the paint, powder and

The Cold War, built by Raccia Motorcycles for Ryan Reynolds.

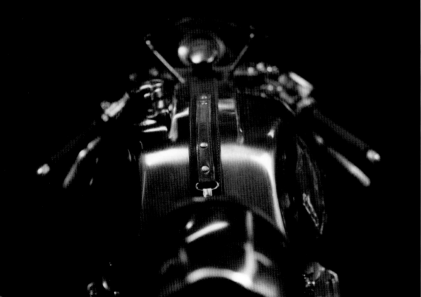

polish. That way you are truly designing something that is based on its engineering, proportions and lines. As long as I have been building two-wheeled engines this is what I have strived to be noted for, not all the added bling. I have no interest in marinating a motorcycle in copper and brass till it becomes attractive like fish to a lure. Icing is the easy part, I want to be known for the cake, and this project was going to be the outlet for that. It became clear to me that this had to be a completely raw machine. I contacted Ryan and he was game.

'As the project progressed so did my passion for making it rawer. I live near a part of Los Angeles that in the 1950s, '60s and '70s was the centre of the world's aerospace industry. Now it is a dried up wasteland of what was. There are still pockets of remnants that remain from that Cold War space race era to pull inspiration. I wanted this machine to feel like exactly that, a machine. A term often used in this recent revival of the café racer is 'cockpit', but I wanted this motorcycle to not just say it, but mean it. I set out to create a motorcycle that actually felt (the closest a motorcycle can feel) like an old warplane cockpit.

'The cockpit is designed after a vintage plane. I made the tachometer to emulate a real fighter plane's gauge. A handful of the nuts, bolts and other small pieces are directly from old fighter planes. I created the fairing with a more angular approach to again give an aerospace feel. Someone once told me a story about the SR-71 Blackbird. During the testing, they once flew one so high in the atmosphere that it fried the paint right off it. When it landed, it was bare metal with only traces of the old logos. I loved that, and wanted to incorporate that aged war-torn look into the design. As for the function itself, well that was a feat of its own.

'Ryan had expressed that this was to be a daily rider, so I knew it had to compete with his other bikes. He has a lot of modern bikes, and he is accustomed to that kind of reliable performance. A stock CB 750 could have been like the runt of the litter, so the motor was given a daily regimen of steroids and gym sessions. A good visual would be the Russian workout scene from Rocky 5. An 836-race piston, high-performance cam, ported and polished, etc. Oh, and, of course, the powerpacking.'

SPEC:

'An enormous amount of mods to the stock front end. Works shocks make this bike feel like a mattress. Works are the best shocks in the galaxy! Buchanan's spokes, the world's greatest spokes, just ask Jupiter. They are a sponsor too, so gotta throw the love.

'Excel high shouldered race rims, also from Buchanan's, who also laced, trued, mounted and balanced the wheels; so it is physically impossible to get a better wheel. Avon tyres, a handmade oil tank, an unspeakable amount of hours modifying that KZ1000 gas tank, handmade fender, custom double-cradled, track-ready race frame and a handmade seat.

'Then I contacted Ryan about getting his hands dirty and picking out the leather for the seat. He contacted me and said, "I have an idea, I'm gonna send you the jacket from the movie I was just in."

"Sweet," I thought to myself. The jacket arrived soon after and I couldn't help but try it on. It felt like pouring maple syrup on hot pancakes; it was so smooth. I am a man of humble desires, so I had never seen a jacket so nice. I looked up the brand online and it turns out it was made by some high end designer in New York. Truly one of the hardest aspects of this build was cutting up that jacket. It took me forty-five minutes to make the first cut.'

History and Build Sheet for the Kawasaki W1R

Michael, tell us about the build:

'About nine years ago, I came across a photo that would haunt me for nearly a decade. It was an old blurry black and white photo on the web of a motorcycle that I had never heard of. I have been building race and race-inspired motorcycles for my entire adult life, so stumbling upon a factory race machine I had never heard of was something I'm not used to. It was the Kawasaki W1R, a race version of the Kawasaki W1650, which was a pretty rare motorcycle itself. This bike was Kawasaki's first attempt to break into the larger displacement motorcycle market in North America. The W1650 was a very close copy of the BSA A-10, and although it had many upgrades and improvements compared to the A-10, its sales were poor and its production run was minimal. After discovering the photo online, I immediately broke out a perimeter search manhunt that even Tommy Lee

Raccia's Kawasaki featuring open clutch drive.

Jones himself would be proud of. I scoured up and down the net looking for more information on this elusive race machine but all I could find were crumbs. I even had a Japanese friend of mine dig through most of the Japanese websites' archives but nothing there either. There is almost no literature on this bike, and one old worn out dusty photo I found was the only one out there.

'From the moment I laid eyes on it, my imaginative and creative wheels were turning, and I knew I had to get my hands on a W1. The idea came to me almost immediately. In the past, my forté had always been to take Japanese motorcycles and recreate them to look more reminiscent of the coveted British and Italian race bikes of the past, but with the limitations of only using OEM Japanese parts. That way the bike would still technically be Japanese. For example, one of my previous CB550 builds was a collage of different factory parts from the big four. The motor is Honda, the gas tank Kawasaki, the front brake is Suzuki and the fender Yamaha, etc. The rules have always been the same for me: it has to be an OEM part that I can modify to appear more vintage racing-esq or something I make from scratch. Never anything aftermarket. So when I stumbled upon the W1R I quickly realised that this was my opportunity to take my ideology a step further. I decided to restrict myself to only using OEM Kawasaki parts, so the bike would for all intents and purposes be a true-blooded Kawasaki. I knew I was destined to attempt to recreate the W1R but there was a small problem: there was no real possibility of making a true replica due to the lack of info and

because the photo was so fuzzy and the original parts were so indecipherable. I decided to fill in the gaps with my favourite GP race bike of all time, the Matchless G45. Just like in Jurassic Park when they used frog DNA to fill in the gaps when creating the dinosaurs, I would do the same with one of the iconic race machines of all time! So the stage was set. I would recreate this mystery machine while at the same time attempting to create the most classically British-looking all Japanese motorcycle ever made ... simple right? Well seven years and more thousands of dollars than I care to mention later, the mission was accomplished.'

The bike was completed using parts from twenty-five different Kawasaki machines ranging from 1966 to 1975.

Some features:
Tank: Modified 1982 Kawasaki GPZ
Front brake: 1965 Kawasaki W2650
Oil tank: Modified side covers from 1974 Kawasak H1
Handlebars: Modified Kawasaki KZ440
Throttle: Stock Kawasaki F21M Greenstreak
Grips: Stock Kawasaki A7
Front fender: Modified Kawasaki G3
Rear fender: Modified front fender from 66 W1650
Muffler: Modified KZ1000 muffler
    And the list goes on and on ...

'It was by far the most difficult motorcycle I have ever made,' says Michael emphatically. 'I took years to research all the parts necessary to make it, with quite a few parts being quite rare. The hardest part was cutting up rare and pricey OEM parts just to realise they wouldn't work and then having to throw them in the trash. It was quite a frustrating and expensive process to say the least. I probably won't be making a lot of friends at the local VVMJ rally anytime soon! The other daunting task was getting all of the proportions the same as the Matchless G45. There aren't very many out there in the world, so finding one to study wasn't going to be easy. I heard there was one in a museum about two hours from me. Luckily the curator was kind enough to allow me to study the bike and take measurements. Then I spent hours studying and logging every square inch of the historic race machine. In total I had to make three trips to the museum, getting kicked out at closing each time. I think by the third time they were pretty tired of me. An arduous task, but in the end well worth it. Every dimension and measurement of my W1R is in direct relation to the Matchless. From the frame dimensions to the handlebar length, exhaust pipe diameter/length, tank strap, etc. Everything is spec to the original except for the fact that it's all Kawasaki parts.'

AUTO FABRICA

Southend-on-Sea is the home to brothers Bujar and Gazmend Muharremi and their little band of metal warriors. I am happy to say, and I am sure they are too, that their order book is full. Their build philosophy – they all have one – is 'keep it simple and therefore beautiful'. Nevertheless, the complexity and sophistication of the build still lies there, it's just skilfully concealed within the remaining components of the bike. They label their creation '*Types*' and Type 6 is an elegant example of their craft. The donor bike in this case was an unloved Yamaha XS650 that the brothers discovered on a farm in rural Cornwall. 'A lucky find that effectively kick-started our company,' said workshop owner Bujar. 'We strived to achieve a bike which was perfectly executed, and epitomised what we saw as a "real" custom motorcycle.'

The guys spend a tremendous amount of time doing preliminary drawings, which just goes to show that every company has its own little way of creation. Some plonk an engine on a bench, others go straight to the computer, while Bujar and Co. commence with simple drawings before switching to Photoshop. They then create the bike in the virtual world before the 'baby' comes to life in the real one.

Bujar says:

'We spend a lot of time balancing clean graphics with highly complex and organic surfaces to achieve a clean yet interesting design. The bike's top line, the shape that the eye rests on first, is made up of the fuel tank and seat, in this case a single gently curving unit made from one piece of 2.5mm aluminium.'

Spec:

Removal of all that is unnecessary
Lowered headstock
Increased rake
AF-stamped leather seat
Rebuilt engine with oversize pistons
2 into 1 custom-made exhausts with inbuilt silencing system, to give the right sound
Hagon rear shocks
Avon 19in and Firestone 18in tyres
Laverda SF750 TLS Front brake hub (very stylish)
Handlebars and controls all AF
Rear wheel built from a standard hub laced to a 19in alloy rim

Bujar continues:

'You can trick the eye by placing the single inlet for the carb on the opposite side to the exhaust port to give a symmetrical balance but it works. To maintain the sleek lines from front to rear we created a metal wrap to go around the clip-ons on yokes. Job done.'

Bujar and Gazmend.

In the workshop.

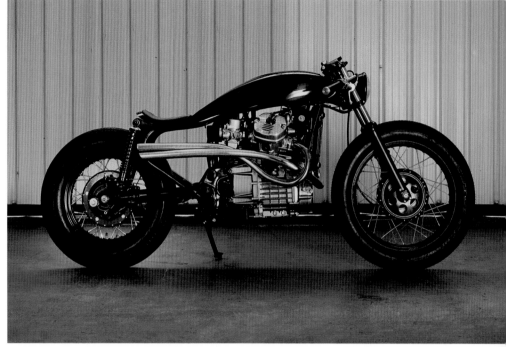

LUDOVIC LAZARETH

FRANCE

And last, but by no means least, we have four fantastic custom builds by Ludovic Lazareth.

Visit YouTube and you will find a few clips of Ludovic and his amazing machines. I can only add my tiny voice to an orchestra of amazement, for the motorcycle industry and movie world have been singing that chorus for some years. For us biking buffs, probably the most incredible bikes from this source appeared in the film *Babylon AD*, featuring Vin Diesel. The critics, and indeed the viewing public, weren't enamoured with the movie, so I guess the stars of that particular production are no doubt the bikes, but I'll let you be the judge of that.

Ludovic Lazareth is French, and I have been so pleased with the international line up of custom bikes and their builders in this book that I may just do a victory roll later on – can you do one of those on a bike? It's got to be worth a try. He and his handful of workers have operated from a small factory in Annecy-le-Vieux near the Swiss border since 1988. Incidentally, have you noticed that in all these successful and creative companies there are only a handful of guys working together? No CEOs and huge corporations, for that would just kill the creative magic.

Included in the line-up is the fantastic, and I use that word in its true context, V8, technically called the LM847. The LM847 is a pendulum four-wheel motorcycle, see what I mean about fantastic? It is powered by a (now we border on the incredible) Maserati V8 470hp engine. Its suspension is kinematic (I have no idea what that means either so you will just have to Google it) which allows the machine to tilt whilst cornering. Just like a bike then! Power is transmitted to the rear wheels via two channels, meanwhile the braking is provided by 8-piston calipers, using discs of 420mm. Moving speedily on to the ridiculous, the bike has only one speed! Power is transmitted by a torque converter that propels you from 0–150kph in seconds. Fancy a go? Nah, nor me; I think I'll give that one a miss.

Yamaha V-Max Hyper Modified

Several of the Big Four, namely Honda; Suzuki; Yamaha and Kawasaki, have in recent years gone seeking partnerships and maybe – though they may not like to admit it openly – inspiration from the small custom

builders. And Yamaha has commissioned three top builders to work their magic on the venerable V-Max 'power cruiser'.

The changes to the bike are relatively toned down, but that's probably due to the design instruction. The version we're looking at here comes from Lazareth, who as we have seen so far likes to operate at the more extreme end of the custom field, and he seems to love bolting superchargers on to his bikes. The bike has been kitted out with an LCD screen with a rear-view video link, just like a recent Kawasaki H1 I saw the other day at the Bridgnorth Café. There's no supercharger this time. Changes include new air intakes and headlight, a new radiator and chin scoop and tail section, and different exhaust system.

FZR Turbo

This prototype fighter also appeared in the movie *Babylon AD* by Mathieu Kassovitz. Is it a sports bike, or is it a dragster? Whatever it is, it's iconic of the company image with its stretched wheelbase; VFR shortened fork and FZR engine, complete with an added Fiat Uno Turbo – just in case the FZR doesn't have enough power! And then there are the aggressively streamlined fairings; and with the addition of a set of sweptback wings, this thing could probably fly too. This piece of kit is a truly sculpted beast, no machine guns, but a true demonstration of what Lazareth and his two-wheeled imagination can achieve.

The Dokujya (on the next page) is another incredible bike from the Lazareth stable, created for the film *Babylon AD*. Now I love red bikes, but I think that this one truly has its butt in the air more than your average sports bike. The machine has been stripped to its minimal, giving a clean look; and that Honda VTR, fitted with a Mini Cooper Supercharger looks fabulous from any angle – mean and menacing. This bike would look great in any colour. Not sure if I'm keen on the single sided front fork, but the aluminium frame is spot on.

The Dokujyalooking
mean and menacing in
bold red.

The Yamaha F2R Turbo by Lazareth Auto Moto.

If you enjoyed this book, you may also be interested in …

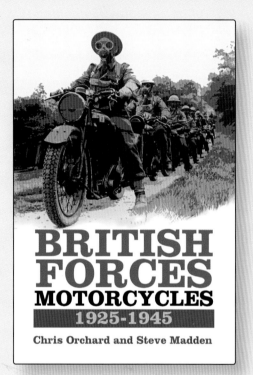

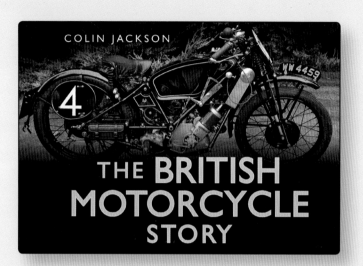

British Forces Motorcyles 1925–1945
CHRIS ORCHARD AND STEVE MADDEN

978 0 7509 7023 5

The British Motorcycle Story
COLIN JACKSON

978 0 7524 8735 9